The Gadfly Papers

Three Inconvenient Essays by One Pesky Minister

Todd F. Eklof

The Gadfly Papers

Three Inconvenient Essays by One Pesky Minister

Todd F. Eklof

Independently Published
Spokane, WA

ISBN: 9781070524481

For Unitarian Universalists

CONTENTS

PREFACE

I don't wish to be a pest. I prefer to get along with people, especially with other Unitarian Universalists, my tribe, and don't enjoy engaging in conflict—not at all! Still, as I must often remind myself, I don't like offending others, but I also don't mind it. What I mean is that I can't allow my wish to get along excuse me to simply go along. I must say what I believe is true and do what I believe is right, even if I'm wrong, and even if doing so isn't going to be fun. I do so humbly but boldly because that's my job as a UU minister and it's also integral to who I am. For whatever reasons, I've become a person who values the freedom of conscience and its expression more than much else. I believe it's a right that should be guaranteed for everyone and one that everyone should respect. I believe we should all protect this right, including for those with whom we may vehemently disagree. This probably explains why I'm a Unitarian Universalist to begin with, because, until recently, I thought freedom of conscience and freedom of speech was *our* thing, too. I'm pretty sure it has been, but, as the essays I've written herein will show, not so much anymore.

The first essay outlines several examples of the suppressive behaviors increasingly being employed within the Unitarian Universalist Association's culture. Borrowing from the framework laid out in *The Coddling of the American Mind* by Greg Lukianoff and Jonathan Haidt, I discuss how some of the same disturbing trends we've seen occurring on college campuses during recent years are now manifesting in the UUA. I suspect most Unitarian Universalists will be surprised by much of what I reveal, which is my intent, so we can make a course correction before it's too late. So far what's been going on has been mostly limited to UUA events, meetings, and publications, though it's increasingly impacting the UU Ministers Association (UUMA), our UU theological schools (Starr King and Meadville-Lombard), the Ministerial Fellowship Committee (MFC), and our Liberal Religious Educator's Association (LREDA), which means the same mindset and behaviors will soon sweep through our pulpits, RE departments, and, alas, our congregations, if those of us who care do nothing.

My second essay discusses the history and difficulties related to the 1961 merger of the Unitarians and the Universalists. In it, I address the unresolved differences between the two faiths, which I suspect are partly to blame for the denominational *identity crisis* we've been in ever since. This crisis, in my opinion, has led to the displacement of Universalism by the emerging culture of *safetyism*, *political correctness*, and *identitarianism* (explained in my first essay). Unitarianism, on the other hand, has become the silent partner in the relationship, pressured by the fear of being publicly shamed for saying anything others might deem harmful or dangerous, or has simply been quietly ignored, uninvited, or disinvited by the UUA's unwritten policies, under the guise of "institutional change." Unitarians must now keep the values closest to their hearts quietly to themselves—freedom of conscience, reason, and the recognition of our common humanity.

I further propose, since Unitarians and Universalists have been unable to accomplish our primary purpose for joining together, establishing a universal religion of humanity for liberal religions around the world, that it may be time to break up. Universalism has died and been displaced by a grotesque imposter in its place. Unitarianism, though muted, still lives, but must break free from the bonds that now restrain it if it is going to survive.

My third essay demonstrates the use of reason, one of Unitarianism's three legs, which Unitarian Universalism still claims is supposed to "warn us against idolatries of mind and spirit." Yet the UUA's response to accusations it upholds racism and white supremacy after a controversial hiring decision in 2017 has been rooted in emotional thinking, not upon substantiated facts or sound reason. Nevertheless, the organization has, upon face value, accepted these accusations must be true, and has since chosen to practically ignore any other issues going on in our denomination, our congregations, our country, and our world. Any dissenting voices have been hushed or brushed aside, creating a self-perpetuating echo chamber, circular reasoning solidified by unfounded memes the UUA has itself helped invent that claim any such dissent only proves its point.

These are not easy matters to write about, having witnessed the vitriol directed at well meaning individuals who get off script, and knowing some of it is now sure to come my way. Nor will it be easy to read about, if, like me, you love Unitarian Universalism and care deeply about freedom and equality for everyone, especially those who are denied it most. But, in fighting for what we believe in, we cannot allow ourselves to become what we disbelieve in, nor achieve our goals by adopting the cruelties of those we oppose. The end matters, but so do the means. The destination holds our hopes, but the path holds our hearts. I, for one, cannot continue traveling along a path with those who no longer respect the minds and voices of their fellow sojourners. So long as the fire of Unitarianism burns within my breast, and the hope of Universalism gives me strength, nothing shall shut my mouth, nor arrest my testimony... not all the stones in Boston.

THE CODDLING OF THE UNITARIAN UNIVERSALIST MIND

How the Emerging Culture of Safetyism, Identitarianism, and Political Correctness is Reshaping America's Most Liberal Religion

1. Safetyism

In their book, *The Coddling of the American Mind*, authors Greg Lukianoff and Jonathan Haidt write about an alarming and rising number of incidents occurring on U.S. college campuses during which students are pressuring others—their peers, professors, and guest lecturers—not to say anything they deem offensive or harmful, using intimidation and, sometimes, violence to achieve their ends. Troubled by these trends, which have mostly gone under-reported by the mainstream national media and glossed over by college administrators, Lukianoff and Haidt, both educators, attempt to explain why such blatant disregard for the free speech of others, especially by socially progressive students, is increasingly present on college campuses, including, ironically, at UC Berkeley, where the Free Speech Movement began in 1964.

Lukianoff and Haidt have coined a term to describe this belief it is morally correct that some freedoms, especially the free flow of ideas, be sacrificed in the name of safety. "Safetyism," they say, "refers to a culture or belief system in which safety has become a sacred value, which means people become unwilling to make trade-offs demanded by other practical or moral concerns."[1] Safetyism, additionally, extends the traditional understanding of what being safe means. "Their focus on 'emotional safety' leads many of them to believe that… 'one should be safe from not just car accidents and sexual assault but from people who disagree with you.'"[2] Since disagreeable ideas are, thus, considered harmful and injurious in a culture of safetyism, many of its adherents feel justified in using violence to protect themselves and others against dangerous beliefs. As a UC Berkeley Op-ed claimed after a violent protest there, "physically violent actions, if used to shut down speech that is deemed hateful, are 'not acts of violence,' but, rather, 'acts of self-defense.'"[3] Whether violent or not, safetyism reflects a value system that stands in opposition to free speech, not unlike the mindset of those legislators who passed the "Patriot Act" after 9/11, which sacrifices individual freedoms in the name of national security.

---

[1] Lukianoff, Greg and Haidt, Jonathan, *The Coddling of the American Mind,* Penguin Press, New York, NY, 2018, p. 30.
[2] Ibid., p. 30f.
[3] Ibid., p. 86.

In September 2018, for example, when it was learned members of the Westboro Baptist Church (the Topeka, Kansas based church notorious for using inflammatory hate speech) was planning a trip to Spokane, Washington to protest a local university, one understandably upset Facebook member responded by writing, "Sometimes there are no two good sides. That is a fallacy created by white supremacist hierarchy to use the value of free speech to spread hate and oppression. Hate and oppression is never okay." Although historians may explain the origins of free speech differently, the point here is that by conflating the concept of "free speech" with the villainy of "white supremacist hierarchy," the writer justifies disregarding the former to prevent the latter, namely, the evils of "hate and oppression." In denying, further, that "Sometimes there are no two good sides," and, by implication, this is one of those times, the writer further justifies extremist thinking and behavior. In this case, the writer's belief is not only presumed to be right but *righteous*, and, therefore, must be defended, even if doing so means denying the freedoms of those who disagree with the writer's morally absolute "side."

As a Unitarian Universalist minister, I found reading *Coddling* personally disturbing for two reasons. Firstly, learning the details of various incidents of violence and cruelty caused by socially progressive students who feel perfectly justified silencing the voices of others, preventing them from saying things judged to be "harmful" or "dangerous," ought to concern anyone who cares about personal freedom. Secondly, and even more troubling for me, has been recognizing the parallels between what's now happening on college campuses and what's also happening within the Unitarian Universalist Association, even though individual autonomy and freedom of conscience have been essential to its meaning dating at least as far back as 1568 when the Edict of Torda, human history's unprecedented religious toleration law, was issued by King John Sigismund Zápolya, the Unitarian King of Transylvania. Alas, its protections were significantly muted after Sigismund's accidental death and, shortly thereafter, that of his Unitarian Bishop, Ferenc Dávid, who died six months after being indungeoned for violating newly established anti-innovation laws that made it illegal to express novel ideas.

Nonetheless, Unitarians, though declared heretics by both the Catholic and Reformed Churches, have, until only recently, continued to cherish individual freedom of conscience and expression, a sentiment also long shared by the American Universalist tradition as epitomized in the story of its founder, Rev. John Murray. Early in 1770s, the Universalist evangelist found himself pressured to keep his "dangerous" disbelief in Hell to himself. Once, for instance, while preaching at a church on School Street in the center of Boston, his audience was drenched with water and Murray hit with an egg. Days later, while publicly debating a far more traditional minister on the subject, his opponent began pushing, pulling, and kicking Murray, repeatedly saying, "You have said enough, quite enough!" The following Sunday he discovered his pulpit had been doused with an unbearably smelly herb. Not one to be intimidated into silence, Murray began preaching despite the stench, only to have an angry mob outside begin throwing rocks through the church windows. After an enormous chunk barely missed hitting the fortunate preacher, some of his members, fearing for his life, pleaded with him to flee his pulpit. Defiant, Murray courageously replied, "not all the stones in Boston, except they stop my breath, shall shut my mouth, or arrest my testimony."[4]

Such tactics, some disruptive, some violent, are not unlike the incidents *Coddling* describes happening on college campuses in response to unwanted speakers. To offer just one of the book's numerous and disturbing examples: on February 1, 2017, roughly 1,500 demonstrators surrounded a building on the University of California's Berkeley campus to protest the presence of right-wing provocateur, Milo Yiannopoulos, with the goal of preventing him from speaking. They succeeded, according to *Coddling*, by breaking windows, throwing Molotov cocktails, shooting fireworks into buildings, dismantling barricades, throwing rocks at police officers, and other acts of violence and vandalism resulting in more than $500,000 in property damage.[5] In addition, a man carrying a sign stating, "The First Amendment is for Everyone," was punched in the face, leaving him bloodied, along with several others whom "protestors attacked with fists, pipes, sticks, and poles."[6] One such attack was caught on camera when a women wearing an infamous MAGA red cap was peppered sprayed while being interviewed by a reporter. In another instance, a student journalist, who afterward described himself as a "moderate liberal," was attacked for recording the event on his cellphone. "When he fled, they chased him, punching

---

[4] Murray, John, *Record of the Life of Rev. John Murray, Monroe and Francis, Boston, MA, 1816.*
[5] Lukianoff & Haidt, ibid., p. 81.
[6] Ibid., p. 82.

him in the head, beating him with sticks, and calling him a 'neo-Nazi.'"[7]

Lukianoff and Haidt describe other examples of such suppression, from milder to worse, having occurred on the campuses of Middlebury College, Claremont McKenna College, College of William and Mary, University of Oregon, Reed College, Rhodes University, University of Tennessee, University of Pennsylvania, and Evergreen State College, between September 2016 and August 2017, though attempts to "disinvite" unwanted speakers have been exponentially accelerating since 2000. "Something began changing on many campuses around 2013," *Coddling* says, "and the idea that college students should not be exposed to 'offensive' ideas is now a majority on campus."[8] According to a 2017 survey, "58% of college students said it is 'important to be part of a campus community where I am not exposed to intolerant or offensive ideas.'"[9]

Safetyism, further, is rooted in several cognitive distortions identified in *Coddling*, some of which are also manifesting in the UUA. I shall discuss some of these instances in more detail as this article proceeds. First, however, it is necessary to understand safetyism's deeper rootedness in *identitarianism*.

2. Identitarianism

Perhaps it should not be surprising the same mindset denounced in *Coddling* is increasingly shared by members

---

[7] Ibid.
[8] Ibid., p. 48.
[9] Ibid.

of the Unitarian Universalist Association, nor unexpected that it's being coddled to by the Association's administration and leadership. This is so because American Unitarianism, in particular, has long been modeled upon and retained much in common with American universities, given many of its original ministers were also college professors and administrators. This is why our credentialed ministers still receive "Fellowship" (an academic term) into the UU Ministers Association, why they take sabbaticals every few years, like college professors, and why, until only recently, our congregations shut down during summer, just as university classes do. Today many ministers continue taking summers off, though our churches are increasingly becoming year-round.

More pertinent to this discussion, though, is that Unitarian Universalism, like American universities, is a mostly liberal institution. Among college professors, as *Coddling* points out, "the [politically] left-to-right ratio was between two to one and four to one from the 1930s through the mid 1990s, but then began to shoot upward, reaching seventeen to one by 2016."[10] This corresponds with the same period liberalism began retreating deeper into University life after its political party of choice lost its prowess during the 1980's Reagan Era, followed by the historic loss of both the House and the Senate to conservative Republicans in 1995, which, at the time, had occurred only once since 1933, and even then lasted only four years. As Humanities Professor, Mark Lilla, explains in his bestseller, *The Once and Future Liberal*, this is also the time a renewed emphasis on identity politics began:

---

[10] Ibid., p. 111.

7

What is astonishing during the Reagan Dispensation was the development of a left-wing version of it that became the de facto creed of two generations of liberal politicians, professors, schoolteachers, journalists, movement activists, and officials of the Democratic Party.[11] ...You may have thought, faced with the dogma of radical economic individualism that Reaganism normalized, liberals would have used their positions in our educational institutions to teach young people that they share a destiny with all their fellow citizens and have duties toward them. Instead, they trained students to be spelunkers of their own personal identities and left them incurious about the world outside their heads.[12]

In short, Lilla says, "Identity is Reaganism for Lefties."[13]

Identity politics, or, "identity liberalism," as Lilla more broadly calls it, and what I mean by, *identitarianism*, refer to the promotion of the interests of certain marginalized or oppressed groups without regard for broader issues than their own, or for the greater concerns of the larger political party or society to which such groups belong. The Brookings Institution, as Lukianoff and Haidt point out, defines it as, "Political mobilization organized around group characteristics such as race, gender, and sexuality, as opposed to party, ideology, or pecuniary interest."[14]

---

[11] Lilla, Mark, *The Once and Future Liberal*, HarperCollins Publishers, New York, NY, 2017, p. 9.
[12] Ibid., p. 60.
[13] Ibid., p. 95.
[14] Lukianoff & Haidt, p. 59.

The result of identitarianism often ends up being a segregated, fractured organization or society that becomes unable to come together to work on its common concerns as a united political force. Hence the election of Donald Trump, who, in 2016, garnered no more votes that Mitt Romney did when he ran against President Obama in 2012. What made the difference for him is that Trump ran against a candidate who many liberals couldn't look beyond their own interests or personal disappointment to vote for, especially in the places where doing so would have most counted. Referring to such behavior as, "self-sabotage," Lilla laments, "At a time when liberals need to speak in a way that convinces people from very different walks of life, in every part of the country, that they share a common destiny and need to stand together, our rhetoric encourages self-righteous narcissism."[15]

Today identity liberalism is not only manifesting strongly in universities, but in other liberal organizations and institutions as well, including the Unitarian Universalist Association. This was demonstrated, for instance, during the UUA's 2017 General Assembly in New Orleans, its first gathering following the election of Donald Trump. Yet, instead of focusing on a collective response to the impacts of this shocking political disaster for liberals or ministering to those still experiencing degrees of anxiety and grief just a few months past the election, the assemblage dwelt almost exclusively on internal accusations of racism and white supremacy resulting from a hiring decision. Although this matter surely needed to be addressed, even more thoroughly and honestly than it was, so did what was going on outside

---

[15] Lilla, ibid., p. 102.

the UU world at the time, especially in light of Trump's victory. Yet such a singular focus should not be surprising if, as Lilla writes, "Every advance of liberal *identity* consciousness has marked the retreat of liberal *political* consciousness."[16]

Solely emphasizing one issue, or one group's issues, is precisely the limitation of engaging in identity politics. If not working in solidarity with other groups identifying with more common issues, efforts are unlikely to have enough collective support to be effective. "The paradox of identity liberalism," Lilla says, "is that it paralyzes the ability to think and act in a way that would actually accomplish the things it professes to want."[17] In short, the splintering and segregation identitarianism inevitably leads to, dooms it to failure. As Wendell Berry puts it, "the social and cultural pluralism some now see as a goal is a public of destroyed communities."[18]

The 2017 UUA General Assembly is not the first time Unitarianism, in particular, has faced the specter of identity liberalism. In the first decades of the 20th century, Unitarian minister, John Haynes Holmes, an early advocate of the Social Gospel and pacifism, credited as the person who made Americans aware of what Gandhi was accomplishing in India at the time, expressed concern his liberal tradition was more concerned about the individual than the social welfare of all individuals, that is, of society as a whole. "The liberal seeks to save [oneself] by culture,

---

[16] Lilla, ibid., p. 10.
[17] Ibid., p. 14.
[18] Berry, Wendell, *Sex, Economy, Freedom, and Community*, Pantheon, New York, NY, 1993, p. 169.

10

education, and development as an individual," and, "seeks to save other people in the same way as individuals."[19] But beyond this, he complained, one "does not go."

Holmes, by contrast, stressed a social gospel in antithesis to orthodox Christianity's emphasis on saving individual souls, believing, "strictly speaking, there is no such thing as an individual at all; that what seems to be an isolated personal entity, embodying its own individual attributes and presenting its own individual problems, is in reality a social creature."[20] Holmes wanted Unitarianism to stand in contrast to such orthodoxy, but regretted, instead, "Liberalism is at one with Catholicism and Protestantism in seeing in each individual nothing but an isolated personal identity, having little or no vital connection with anything or anyone external to itself."[21]

Nearly two centuries before Holmes wrote these words, other liberal ministers were stressing the need for religion to shift its attention away from the interests of the individual. This notion was such a shift in thinking that it had to have its own name. Placing greater emphasis upon society and human welfare was sometimes referred to as "Liberal Christianity" or "Liberal Protestantism." The political activist and socialist theologian, Fredrich Naumann coined the term, "Practical Christianity." William Ellery

---

[19] Holmes, John Haynes, *The Revolutionary Function of the Modern Church*, G.P. Putnam's Sons, New York, NY, 1912, p. 34.
[20] Holmes, ibid., p. 38. [For those interested in learning more about the philosophical problems of identity, which is beyond the scope of this essay, I highly recommend both, *The Ethics of Identity* and *The Lies that Bind*, by Kwame Anthony Appiah, *Identity*, by Francis Fukuyama, and *The Once and Future Liberal*, by Mark Lilla.]
[21] Ibid., p. 28f.

Channing named it, "Unitarianism." As Historian Helena Rosenblatt, explains in her book, *The Lost History of Liberalism*, "Each one of these liberal Protestants believed that the Christian religion should rid itself of what they thought was a narrow, negative, and excessively narrow individualistic attitude that focuses on saving each person's soul, and devote itself to bettering the lives of all people."[22] This is why, Rosenblatt says, "Some liberals said that Unitarianism could lead people to an even better religion, namely the, 'Religion of Humanity.'"[23]

3. The Religion of Humanity

When, during the first decades of the 20th century, radical Unitarian ministers like John H. Dietrich and Curtis W. Reese suggested their denomination become less theistic and more humanistic, they sparked a long controversy within Unitarianism that became known as the *Humanist Debate*. But an even longer view of history shows Unitarianism has always been humanistic at its core, and, for this reason, formal Humanism was bound to eventually emerge from it.

Unitarianism, after all, existed informally in the first centuries of Christianity as the belief in Jesus's humanity and his humanitarian teachings. It was in reaction against this original idea (then called *Arianism*) that Rome, which had appropriated Christianity from its original monotheistic Jewish followers, adopted the Nicaean Creed in 325 CE, effectively declaring Jesus a god. 56 years later, during the

---

[22] Rosenblatt, Helena, *The Lost History of Liberalism*, Princeton University Press, Princeton, NJ, 2018, p. 235.
[23] Ibid., p. 153.

Council of Constantinople, Church authorities added the Holy Spirit to the mix, officially establishing the Trinitarian Doctrine, while making Christianity's original Unitarian belief in Jesus's humanity illegal. This, in turn, led to a profound theological shift from seeing a human being as worthy to be called a child of God, to, instead, seeing a god lower itself to save human beings from their innate corruption—from human dignity to human depravity.

This remained so throughout the Dark Ages, until the invention of the printing press in 1440 CE, making it possible for more people to read the Bible for themselves. Among them was a young theologian named Michael Servetus who was surprised to find no mention of a Trinity in it. After writing a book about his discovery, Servetus was declared a heretic by Reformer John Calvin who, in 1553, had him tried and burned at the stake, the lethal pyre kindled by Servetus's own writings. By then, however, it was already too late. Unitarianism had been reborn in Eastern Europe, which, as mentioned earlier, soon led to its formal adoption by King Sigismund in 16th century Transylvania.

This awakening included a renewed emphasis upon Jesus's humanity and his humanitarian teachings. When Unitarian Bishop Ferenc Dávid was condemned for violating anti-innovation laws, for example, it was because he was teaching against praying to Christ, whom he considered a human being, not a god. It made no more sense to him for Protestants to pray to Jesus than for Catholics to pray to Mary—a comparison that cost him both his freedom and his life.

Although Dávid's friend, the Italian theologian, Faustus Socinus, had unsuccessfully tried to convince him to alter his position and save his life, he too held a Unitarian theology and was eventually persecuted for teaching that salvation comes, not through Jesus's propitiatory death, but by putting his teachings into practice. Socinus also rejected the doctrine of Original Sin and its idea of human depravity, and was among other early antitrinitarian reformers, Matteo Gribaldi, Gianpaolo, Giovani Gentile, and Giorgio Biandrata, historically referred to as "Italian Humanists."[24]

American Unitarianism emerged independently from Eastern European Unitarianism but did so for much the same reasons, namely, an enlightened rationalism and desire for a less sectarian religion that focuses more on human need and development than on theological beliefs. Like their 16th century European kin, these 18th century American theologians held a positive view of humanity, the kind of humanity they hoped to nurture by establishing a universal religion. Rev. Charles Chauncy, for example, minister of Boston's First Church for 60 years, from 1727 to 1787, stood as chief opponent to Jonathan Edwards, leader of the, so-called, Great Awakening. This opposition included arguing against its "New Birth" movement—the belief human beings are born in sin and "must be born again," through a religious conversion experience. Chauncy argued human beings are born, "with the capacity for both sin and righteousness,"[25] an idea that, at the time, was called *Arminianism*, the precursor of what was to become American Unitarianism.

A hundred years later, sometime after Chauncy's Congregational church officially became Unitarian, this

---

[24] Howe, Charles A., *For Faith and Freedom*, Skinner House Press, Boston, MA, 1997, p. 56.
[25] Robinson, David, *The Unitarians and the Universalists*, Greenwood Press, Westport, CT, 1985, p. 11.

belief in human goodness, or, rather, the disbelief in human depravity, was expressed by the Unitarian minister John Haynes Holmes, whom, again, as an early advocate of the Social Gospel, believed religion should concentrate on human welfare and agency, not upon "the supernatural and the miraculous."[26] In the early 1900s, Universalist minister Clarence Skinner, one of Holmes' younger associates, also began emphasizing the Social Gospel and, with it, a positive view of human nature. Skinner penned a Declaration of Social Principles and Social Program adopted by the Universalist General Convention in 1917 that explicitly rejected the idea of "inherent depravity," claiming instead, "that mankind is led into sin by evil surroundings, by the evils of unjust social and economic systems."[27] It went on to call for the basic right to own land, equal rights for women, freedom of speech, some form of social security for everyone, and a global government guaranteeing these same rights for everyone, everywhere. In his book *Liberalism Faces the Future*, Skinner said the starting point of liberalism must be a sense that, "at the core of human nature is something good and sound... [an] inherent moral capacity to choose the right..."[28]

Likewise, in 1911, at the start of the 20th century, after being the first and only minister ever convicted of heresy by the Dutch Reformed Church, John H. Dietrich was invited to occupy the Unitarian pulpit in Spokane, Washington. It was there, upon reading the word afresh in a book given him by one of its members, Dietrich first called

---

[26] Ibid., p. 137.
[27] Ibid., p. 140.
[28] Ibid., p. 141.

himself a "Humanist," with a capital *H*. His conversion should come as no surprise given the newfound ideological freedom afforded him by the Spokane Unitarian Society, which was unusually radical, even by Unitarian standards. Its 1888 bylaws, adopted less than a year after the congregation's establishment, stated, "the authority for its belief is reason; The method of finding its beliefs is scientific; Its aim is to crush superstition and establish facts of religion;" and its, "First principle is freedom of opinion and is subject to no censure for heresy..."[29] The book he'd been given contained an article on Auguste Comte's philosophy of Positivism, which Dietrich "loosely defined as the religion of humanity,"[30] but the article's author had shortened to just "humanism." It was then, according to his biographer, Dietrich realized, "This age honored word, this 'humanism' would be a good name for his interpretation of religion in contrast to theism."[31]

Dietrich remained in Spokane five years before accepting a call to the Unitarian Society of Minneapolis where he established the Humanist Pulpit, became known as the "Father of Religious Humanism," and, with his friend Curtis W. Reese, a Southern Baptist convert to the Unitarian ministry, became signers of the original *Humanist Manifesto* in 1933. Indeed, almost half the manifesto's original 34 signers were Unitarians.

Even in light of this long history, in which Unitarianism has remained almost synonymous with

---

[29] McDowell, Esther, *Unitarians in the State of Washington*, Frank McCaffrey Publishers, 1966. p. 97.
[30] Winston, Carleton, *The Circle of Earth: The Story of John H. Dietrich*, G.P. Putnam's Sons, New York, NY, 1942, p. 122.
[31] Ibid.

humanistic theology, or, at least, a humanistic Christology, the efforts of Dietrich and Reese to make it less sectarian led to much debate. As *The Dictionary of Modern American Philosophers* explains, "It took over a decade and a half for Unitarians to decide they could tolerate humanists, not only in their church pews, but in their pulpits as well."[32] "Tolerate," however, may be an understatement given the results a survey submitted in 1967, which the Unitarian Universalist Association had begun working on only a few years after the two denominations merged in 1961, with the aim of profiling the "typical Unitarian Universalist."[33] Of the 12,000 members surveyed, from 800 congregations, less than 3 percent claimed to believe in a "supernatural being," 28 percent considered God "an irrelevant concept," 57 percent did not consider theirs a "Christian" religion, and 52 percent preferred "a distinctive humanistic religion."[34]

It is in light of this historical backdrop that Unitarian Universalism remains well situated to respond to the current wave of identity liberalism and its divisive repercussions by rediscovering its deepest roots, highest aspirations, and still unfulfilled mandate to establish a religion of humanity. This is not to suggest Unitarian Universalism should not continue concerning itself with those grave issues of injustice impacting specific groups, only that doing so requires a corresponding emphasis upon our common humanity. As philosopher Philip E. Devine writes in *Human Diversity and the Culture Wars*, "dealing with human diversity requires a

---

[32] Shook, John R., *The Dictionary of Modern American Philosophers*, Thoemmes Continuum, Great Britain, 2005, p. 647.
[33] Robinson, ibid., p. 176.
[34] Ibid., p. 177.

shared conception of our common humanity and that the more aware we are of the pervasiveness of diversity, the more important such a conception of human nature will be."[35] In other words, the more we focus on our differences, the more we must also pay attention to that which makes us one, lest what we do in the name of diversity lead us only deeper into division.

Decades before Dr. Martin Luther King, Jr. famously said, "All men are caught in an inescapable network of mutuality, tied in a single garment of *destiny*," John H. Dietrich spoke similarly of "the divine thrill of the shared life as we strive together toward our common destiny,"[36] and Curtis Reese, conversely, considered, "self-culture, pursued as an end in itself, to be a potentially hazardous diversion of energy away from social connection."[37]

Certainly, as Devine cautions, "In our attempt to discover our common humanity, we need to avoid treating our own peculiarities as definitive of human nature, a failure to which the privileged are perhaps peculiarly subject."[38] Yet, as he also insists, "The resolution of cultural conflicts requires more than anything else a recognition of the shared humanity of everyone involved."[39] This is so, as humanism presumes, because our differences can only be appreciated, supported, and celebrated, rather than feared, suppressed,

---

[35] Devine, Philip E., *Human Diversity and the Culture Wars*, Praeger Publishers, Westport, CT, 1996, p. 153.
[36] Dietrich, John H., *What if the World Went Humanist? Ten Pulpit Addresses by John H. Dietrich*, The HUUmanists Association, Hamden, CT., 2010, p. 104.
[37] Robinson, ibid., p. 145.
[38] Devine, ibid., p. 81.
[39] Ibid., p. 120.

and demonized, when we recognize they are rooted in our common humanity, like different spokes radiating from a shared hub, or branches from one tree. It is our common humanity that is, to paraphrase the *Bhagavad Gita*, "the thread that runs through the pearls, as in a necklace."[40]

In discussing a dialectic view of human history, which the 18th century German philosopher, Georg Wilhelm Friedrich Hegel believed was driven by the universal human desire for *thymos* (recognition), Francis Fukuyama reminds us Hegel believed, "the only rational solution to the desire for recognition was universal recognition, in which every human being was recognized"[41] Yet Fukuyama goes on to point out, "Universal recognition has been challenged ever since by other partial forms of recognition based on nation, religion, sect, race, ethnicity, or gender, or by individuals wanting to be recognized as superior."[42] Such divisions, when loosed from the recognition of our common humanity, are like scattered pearls fallen from a broken thread, leading to the kind of divisive identity politics that is now spreading all of us, especially liberals, further apart.

4. Concept Creep

In the Spring 2019 *UU World* magazine, an article appeared entitled "After L, G, and B." Its description stated that, "Listening to transgender and nonbinary people is about

---

[40] Fox, Matthew, *One River, Many Wells*, Jeremy P. Tarcher/Putnam, New York, NY, 2000, p. 18

[41] Fukuyama, Francis, *Identity: The Demand for Dignity and the Politics of Resentment*, Farrar, Straus and Giroux, New York, NY, 2018., p. xvi.

[42] Ibid.

respect, relationship, and whether Unitarian Universalism can be the welcoming faith we claim." Its author speaks of her own lessons learned while relating to her daughter's transgender girlfriend; explains the different meanings of *transgender, binary, intersex,* and *queer*; discusses some of the challenges nonbinary citizens face in the U.S.; the discomfort many trans UUs feel finding a comfortable and supportive home in Unitarian Universalist congregations; and closes by stressing the importance of getting the language right when addressing and supporting persons who are transgender.

You may be surprised to learn this well-intentioned article was received with much outrage, enough that UUA President Rev. Susan Frederick-Gray issued a prompt apology, stating, "More than anything, I want to acknowledge the harm and pain this article is creating," further explaining she had also instructed the magazine's editor to issue an additional apology, which he entitled, "Our Story Hurt People." Some Facebook posts on the matter also used words like *harm, hurt,* and *pain* to describe its impact.

In *Coddling,* Lukianoff and Haidt specifically discuss how "concept creep" has expanded the meaning of "harm" and its synonyms (i.e., hurt, pain, injury, trauma) to also mean "feelings." Citing a 2016 article entitled, "Concept Creep: Psychology's Expanding Concepts of Harm and Pathology," written by psychologist Nick Haslam, they note that concepts like "abuse, bullying, trauma, and prejudice" began changing in the 1980s, having "crept 'downward,' to apply to less severe situations, and 'outward,' to encompass new but conceptually related phenomena."[43] In addition, the right to declare something is "harmful" or "traumatic" shifted from strict, objective criteria, as listed in the DSM,[44] for example, to a *"subjective standard."*[45]

Since one's subjective experience of words is now enough to deem them harmful, and, therefore, dangerous, those who speak are pressured to consider the "safety" of those they communicate with their top priority. "…the notion of 'safety' underwent a process of 'concept creep' and expanded to include *'emotional* safety,'" *Coddling* says, as exemplified in a 2014 memo Oberlin College administrators posted requesting their faculty use trigger warnings to "show students that you care about their safety," and that simply using the wrong pronoun "prevents or impairs their safety in the classroom."[46] This explanation of concept creep, particularly regarding notions of what it means to be "harmed" and to be "safe," helps explain the angry and defensive reaction to the well-intended *UU World* article.

"There is a principle in philosophy and rhetoric called the principle of charity," *Coddling* further reminds us, "which says that one should interpret other people's statements in their best, most reasonable form, not in the worst or most offensive way possible."[47] Although this principle has long been practiced among Unitarian Universalists, part of the covenantal relationships we agree to in many of our congregations, at least one individual was

---

[43] Lukianoff and Haidt, ibid., p. 25.
[44] Diagnostic Statistical Manuel
[45] Lukianoff & Haidt, ibid., p. 26.
[46] Ibid., p. 24f.
[47] Ibid., p. 55.

angry enough to insist the magazine's editor tender his immediate resignation over the matter.

The main issue with it, for those troubled by it, is that it was written by a nontrans woman. As one post stated, "the cis-white gaze is strong in UU world." Another said, "As the mother of a trans person, I must say I was appalled. You are right; we can do better. Let's make sure that when we make space for people's voices, that they are speaking for themselves." (This comment, ironically, seems to violate the writer's own mandate.)

Such an ethic may make sense in light of identity liberalism, which predictably leads to precisely this kind of schism, in which those identifying with specific groups become incapable of relating to those outside their tribal identity. "What replaces argument, then, is taboo..." Lilla says. "Only those with an approved identity status are, like shamans, allowed to speak on certain matters."[48] Yet even if this were so, as Kwame Anthony Appiah writes in *The Lies that Bind*, "Having an identity doesn't, by itself, authorize you to speak on behalf of everyone of that identity."[49]

The humanistic ethic, on the other hand, recognizes we are fundamentally one, which is precisely why we must all be treated with respect and why it is the responsibility of us all to advocate for those among us who are not. "If we want to create welcoming, inclusive communities," Lukianoff and Haidt say, "we should be doing everything we can to turn down the tribalism and turn up the sense of common humanity."[50]

---

[48] Lilla, ibid., p. 91.
[49] Appiah, Kwame Anthony, *The Lies that Bind*, Liveright Publishing Corporation, New York, NY, 2018, p. 19.
[50] Lukianoff & Haidt, ibid., p. 70.

In this spirit, it seems pertinent to mention the same *UU World* issue contained a second article, immediately following "After L, G, and B," that was, indeed, written and submitted by the Steering Committee of the Trans Religious Professional Unitarian Universalists Together (TRUUsT). Entitled, "A Call to Action," it points out specific data indicating only "28 percent of trans UUs feel as though their current or most recent UU experience is completely inclusive of them as trans people," in addition to listing several ways in which congregations can do better in this regard. The implication, then, given the existence of this second article, at least according to those outraged by the first, is that it's now forbidden for anyone to talk about trans issues but trans people, and, by extension, any other identity group by outsiders, no matter how supportive their words might be.

I shall leave it to you to determine the merits of these very different perspectives and close this section by pointing out the linguicidal nature of the conflict, which I shall discuss more fully in the next. For now, respecting freedom of conscience and its expression, whether we agree with what's said or not, has long been a cherished principle of Unitarianism. The puritanical pressures now being instituted by internal denominational forces to control the narrative of others—both who can speak and what they can speak about—and, thus, the overall group mindset, represents a form of oppression Unitarianism has, until now, resisted. Using shame, self-righteousness, and enraged warnings about dangerous ideas and hurtful speech in the name of justice and righteousness, is no less than the excuses some once used to burn Unitarians at the stake, to cast stones at

Universalists as they preached, and to kick them as they tried to debate, insisting, "You have said enough, quite enough!"

5. Linguicide

In ancient Rome, rather than sending people to prison, they were sometimes sent into exile, especially those who expressed minds of their own. As William B. Irvine reminds us in his book *A Guide to the Good Life*, "philosophers were expelled from Rome at least three times: in 161 BC, again during the reign of Emperor Vespasian, and yet again during the reign of Domitian."[51] Stoic philosophers like Seneca and Musonius Rufus, for instance, were exiled to the Island of Gyaros, south of Greece, by Emperor Nero, the same island that "was still being used as a place of banishment in the twentieth century; it is where Greek generals sent their political opponents in the early 1970s."[52]

Banishing those with whom we disagree, or banning them from saying what we disagree with, has been part of social control, in varying forms, for a very long time. Those doing the banishing or banning always feel morally justified doing so because they believe they are squashing or repelling the dangerous and harmful ideas of those they exile, torture, execute, or otherwise silence. From exile and ostracism practiced in ancient Rome, to the Crusades, Inquisitions, heresy trials, and McCarthyism, those responsible have considered it their religious and moral responsibility to

---

[51] Irvine, William B., *A Guide to the Good Life*, Oxford University Press, New York, NY, 2009, p. 183.
[52] Ibid., p. 49.

suppress the "dangerous" voices of those with whom they and their communities disagree.

Indeed, history suggests the first step in subjugating others is suppressing their freedom of speech. This is why *linguistic colonialism* (alt. *language imperialism*) always accompanies the spread of empire. As Spanish grammarian Antonio de Nebrija recognized in 1492, "siempre la lengua fue compariera del imperio"[53] (*language was always the companion of empire*). Or, as British colonialist Edmund Spencer admitted in 1596, "it hath ever been the use of the Conqueror to despise the language of the conquered and to force him by all means to learn his [own]."[54]

This is the reason, after 500 years of British colonialism, English is one of the top three languages in the world, even though England is little more than half the size of California, and why even more people round the globe speak Spanish, though Spain itself is only about as big as Texas. This effort to impose the dominant culture by controlling the language of the oppressed, and, thus, controlling the larger conversation and mindset, is why the ancient Roman Empire forced Latin upon its subjects, and why Japan imposed its language on those it conquered at the start of the 20th century, and why the Chinese are currently forcing Tibetans to speak Mandarin, and why, in our own modern era, governments in Canada, Brazil, South Africa, Australia, and the United States, forcibly and heartlessly removed indigenous children from their homes and placed

---

[53] Crowley, Tony, "Colonialism and Language," The Cambridge Encyclopedia of the Language Sciences, ed. P. Hogan, Cambridge, 2008.
[54] Ibid.

them in institutions where they were punished and abused for speaking their native tongues.

This "linguistic genocide," or, "linguicide," as it's sometimes called, is defined as, "the systematic replacement of an indigenous language with the language of an outside, dominant group, resulting in a permanent language shift and the death of the indigenous language."[55] Linguicide and Linguistic colonialism, however, haven't been the only ways dominant cultures have worked to control speech. The Catholic Inquisition, for instance, was responsible for the persecution and executions of unknown thousands for heresy. *Heresy* comes from the Greek word meaning "choice." Heretics were simply those who chose to express their own ideas, rather than those imposed upon them by the Church. Michael Servetus, the founder of Unitarianism itself, was, again, burned at the stake, along with his writings, for differing with the religious authorities of his day. A shorter time ago, McCarthyism in the U.S. effectively made it illegal to talk about socialism and workers' rights. Those convicted of doing so by the House Un-American Activities Committee could be imprisoned, and those suspected of being communist sympathizers were put on a list that made them ineligible to work.

It is difficult to imagine those claiming to be liberals engaging in such suppression, given that *liberal* comes from the Latin word meaning "freedom," let alone members of the Unitarian Universalist Association, representing the world's

---

[55] Isabelle L´eglise, Bettina Migge, "Language and colonialism. Applied linguistics in the context of creole communities," Marlis Hellinger & Anne Pauwels. Language and Communication: Diversity and Change. Handbook of Applied Linguistics, Mouton de Gruyter, pp. 297-338, 2007.

most liberal religion. Yet, with regard to the article mentioned in the previous section, a UUA staff member sent an almost immediate email addressed to its Pacific Western Region's board presidents and ministers with the subject, "A note about the UU World article 'After L, G and B.'" The email explained, "As the article was being planned and written, multiple transgender people asked that the article not be run, that an article written by someone who is actually transgender would be more appropriate." Again, I shall leave it to my reader to determine if a magazine editor acts improperly by publishing an article after being asked not to. More troubling is the email concluded by instructing its recipients to read a list of complaints about the article and then "actively speak to the harm it does," to "Read and amplify trans UU voices speaking to why this article is so harmful," and asks, "If your gender identity matches the gender you were born into (cisgender) and the article seems fine to you even after reading the links above, please do not ask transgender people in your life to explain it to you. That's a microaggression and it causes harm and exhaustion." The irony of yet another voice speaking for transgender persons about not speaking for transgender persons aside, I leave it to you to decide if it is the place of UUA staff to instruct our congregational presidents and ministers not only how they should think on such issues, but what they should and shouldn't say to whom.

6. Microaggressions & the Callout Culture

The term "micro-aggression" was coined in 1974 by Harvard Medical School professor of psychiatry Chester M. Pierce, in reference to the degrading ways African Americans are portrayed in the mass media "and copied in white-black real life encounters."[56]

> What the reader must bear in mind is that these assaults to black dignity and black hope are incessant and cumulative. Any single one may not be gross. In fact, the major vehicle for racism in this country is offenses done to blacks by whites in this sort of gratuitous, never-ending way. These offenses are micro-aggressions.[57]

In naming this troubling and disturbing social reality, Pierce hoped psychiatry could be used to help African Americans impacted by negative images of themselves to, indeed, change the negative cultural narrative that often gets stuck in their own heads.

> Every community psychiatrist therefore should inform himself of the fundamentals of propaganda so that he can be in an advisory and educative role in helping masses of blacks understand and dilute, if not counteract, the ceaseless brainwashing that goes on via mass communications with the conscious as well as unconscious design to keep blacks ineffective, passive, hopeless, and helpless.[58]

Today "microaggression" has gone through concept creep and been misappropriated by the suppressive cultural

---

[56] Pierce, Chester M., "Psychiatric Problems of the Black Minority," from *American Handbook of Psychiatry: Volume 2*, edited by Silvano Arieti, Basic Books, New York, NY, 1974, p. 16.
[57] Ibid., p. 13.
[58] Ibid., p. 16.

phenomenon known as *political correctness*. Although it is not a stretch to apply the term to any marginalized group that is negatively portrayed in the mainstream media, it's a colossal leap to think the concept can easily be used by anyone to spontaneously psychoanalyze the unconscious minds and motives of others. Pierce coined the term in a professional journal to inform psychiatrists of the phenomenon. It was not meant to be used with abandon by novices who presume it gives them the spontaneous power to immediately know the subconscious intentions of others. "...it is not a good idea to start by *assuming the worst about people* and reading their actions as uncharitably as possible," Lukianoff and Haidt tell us, "This is a [cognitive] distortion known as mind reading."[59]

When applied in this way, the misappropriation and misuse of the term "microaggression" becomes another mechanism for dismissing and silencing the voices of others by openly shaming them and making them chronically anxious about saying anything for fear it might be misconstrued as inappropriate. Referring to this practice as the "callout culture," *Coddling* says, "anyone can be publicly shamed for saying something well-intentioned that someone interprets uncharitably."[60] When used in this way, this misapplication of "microaggression" is not merely a form of mindreading, but of mind control.

Lukianoff and Haidt further suggest the *callout culture* has emerged from the widespread use of social media where "there is always an audience eager to watch people

---

[59] Lukianoff & Haidt, ibid., p. 41.
[60] Ibid., p. 5.

The Gadfly Papers

being shamed, particularly when it is so easy for spectators to join in and pile on."[61] This practice is also becoming widespread on college campuses where entering students are not only learning to spot "microaggressions" during orientation, but how to "gain prestige for identifying small offenses committed by members of their community, and then 'calling out' the offenders."[62] Those seeking such prestige by publicly shaming others is now referred to as *virtue signaling.*

This, understandably, has also led to an emerging pattern of "defensive self-censorship"[63] by those anxious about the possibility of being called out and publicly demonized or humiliated. In addition to making it more challenging for students to "practice the essential skills of critical thinking and civil disagreement,"[64] *Coddling* says, "Many in the audience may feel sympathy for the person being shamed but are afraid to speak up, yielding the false impression that the audience is unanimous in its condemnation."[65] It is based upon a few private conversations I've had with a small number of other Unitarian Universalist ministers that I anecdotally infer this same trepidation also exists among some in the UUA. There are those deeply concerned about what's going on at our Boston headquarters, in our theological schools (Meadville-Lombard and Starr King), during clergy gatherings, and, increasingly, in our congregations, yet are afraid to say anything about it for fear of being ostracized. Yet it is my

[61] Ibid., p. 71f.
[62] Ibid., p. 71.
[63] Ibid., p. 10.
[64] Ibid., p. 10f.
[65] Ibid., p. 72.

30

hope enough of us will find the courage to voice our concerns so our religion might enter into a genuine dialogue about these difficult matters.

During the 2017 General Assembly, for example, delegates voted to end the denomination's "Standing on the Side of Love" campaign "to create a new imaging that better includes and reflects the needs and contributions of disabled people," the motion stated. During discussion of it, one person opposing the motion stated:

> As an able-bodied white male, I approach the microphone with considerable trepidation. As a lover of poetry and religious language, however, I am afraid, afraid that almost any metaphor of human interaction with the world will speak to abilities that not all people share. Since it is about our senses and our bodies that we all interact with the world. Open my eyes that I may see. Lift up mine eyes into the hills. But what if I cannot see? Now, the ears of my ears awake, but what if we cannot hear? Women who run with the wolves. But what of those who cannot run? We just sang a beautiful new version of Jason Shelton's inspiring [song], but still, we sang of "hands joined together on a private new day." What of those who lack hands or for whom the brightness as a metaphor for good is an echo of white supremacy? I do not want in any way to belittle the pain that language so frequently causes. And again, I am very conscious myself of being in the privileged group. But I ask that we consider the possibility that prioritizing inclusiveness may sometimes undermine our ability to powerfully articulate our faith.

Despite the eloquence of this argument, the majority of delegates voted to approve the motion to stop using,

"*Standing* on the Side of Love." The primary point here, however, is the way in which this particular delegate began his statement, "As an able-bodied white male, I approach the microphone with considerable trepidation." Such anxiety about expressing oneself is the end result of the PC culture's linguistic puritanism, as it is meant to be. "Propositions become pure or impure, not true or false," Lilla says. "And not only propositions but simple words:"

> Left identitarians who think of themselves as radical creatures, contesting this and transgressing that, have become like buttoned-up Protestant schoolmarms when it comes the English language, parsing every conversation for immodest locutions and rapping the knuckles of those who inadvertently use them.[66]

In the past, the dread of speaking openly has been associated with other religions, not Unitarian Universalism. Ours has been a faith, rather, in which it has not been acceptable that anyone should have to approach a microphone with fear and trembling.

7. Political Correctness

The appropriated use of "microaggressions" and the *callout culture* are, again, expressions of the larger phenomenon known as political correctness, or, simply, PC, which Philip E. Devine defines as a "militant and intolerant relativism."[67] These unflattering terms are not ones liberals usually

---

[66] Lilla, ibid., p. 91.
[67] Devine, ibid., p. xi.

associate with themselves, but Devine insists, "mainstream liberals" bear considerable responsibility for the PC phenomenon. "For the central strategy of relativistic liberals is to impose silence on positions and arguments that transgress the limitations liberals impose on public discourse."[68]

During the same UUA General Assembly previously mentioned, for instance, a trustee spoke during a General Session of the difficulty the Board had determining how best to fill the position unexpectedly vacated by its President, Peter Morales, after a controversial hiring decision led to his abrupt resignation:

> ...as we were making decisions about how to fill the role of the presidency some of us were blinded. I was blinded by my whiteness. And it was our colleagues on the board of color and others with great wisdom who saw a different way. Had it not been for that vision and had it not been for some mighty-big sunglasses to help with that blindness, why then we would have not wound up with this fabulous group of co-presidents.

After a round of applause for the Board's appointees, followed by a preliminary credentials report, the trustee returned to the microphone with the following awkwardly stated admission:

> I just made a giant mistake. For those of you that have visual problems, I apologize for my analogy to blindness. Sometimes we can see with our eyes. Sometimes we can

---

see with our minds. And my metaphors, please forgive me now for that and I will do better next time.

Having served on the GA Worship Arts Team at the same time this supposed transgression occurred, I was also surprised to learn there are certain songs in the denominational hymnal the UUA now considers inappropriate for us to sing. I was informed, "One More Step," for example, cannot be sung anymore for the same reasons the *Standing on the Side of Love* campaign has been changed to *Side with Love*, because some have determined the word's "step" and "stand" exclude those who cannot walk. I then suggested the hymn, "We'll Build a Land," based upon prophetic statements from the Hebrew scriptures, and later echoed by Dr. King, "Let justice roll down like waters, and righteousness like a mighty stream," but was informed it too is forbidden because the term, "We'll Build a Land" may offend Native Americans.

Here, too, I will leave it to my reader to determine the soundness of banning the singing of songs for such reasons, as well as words like "blinded" and "stand." I will mention, however, that I've been unable to ascertain an official list of banned songs, nor any agreed-upon criteria for determining which songs and hymns should be considered politically incorrect. It is precisely this absence of objective criteria that leads to the kind of *relativism* Philip Devine refers to when defining political correctness. Since its adherents' admonishments are as random and subjective as they are relative, furthermore, those accused of violating their erratic expectations are often left feeling as bewildered as they are unduly chastised. As John William Murray, a former U.S. Representative and U.S. District Judge, once complained of postmodernism in general, the tendency, that is, to reject empirical data in favor of relativistic whims; "postmodernists do not aspire to bask in the pure light of reality, but rather wallow in the mire of opinion. They work with slimy concepts, rather than the rigorous axioms of logic."[69]

Since, and this again is the point, there is no consistency regarding when or how a word might be determined offensive, PC also has a chilling effect on any kind of meaningful dialogue, as, again, is its purpose. "In our identitarian age," Shadi Hamid, of the Brookings Institute, says, "the bar for offence has been lowered considerably, which makes democratic debate more difficult—citizens are more likely to withhold their true opinions if they fear being labeled as bigoted or insensitive."[70]

Hence, within the deafening, though comfortable, echo chamber political correctness fashions for itself, in which its practitioners hear only their own unchallenged and unexamined absolutisms bounced back to themselves, real people are silenced, publicly shamed, demonized, or have their motives and minds uncharitably and unethically psychoanalyzed by those with no qualifications for doing so. "Historically, the conservatives have most often answered the centers with anathemas," Devine reminds us, "but refusal of dialogue is now a hallmark of the cultural left."[71] It also seems to have become a hallmark of our liberal religion, which once prized freedom of conscience, speech, and expression above much else. The unsound and unethical use

---

[69] Devine, ibid., p. 29.
[70] Lukianoff & Haidt, ibid., p. 42.
[71] Ibid., p. 79.

of political correctness to discourage honest dialogue, creating the kind of anxiety and dread of talking that leads to awkward appeals for forgiveness for simply letting a metaphor slip off the tongue, is indicative of a puritanical community, not a liberal one.

Nevertheless, while preparing for its 2019 General Assembly in Spokane, Washington, the UUA pulled a contract only days before it was to be signed by Alice Walker, who had agreed to deliver the event's prestigious Ware Lecture. In a December 2018 *New York Times* article, Walker, a Pulitzer Prize winning author and activist, cited David Icke's book, *And the Truth Shall Set You Free*. Icke is considered both a conspiracy theorist and anti-Semitic by his critics. (Even from what little I know of him; I can understand why.) Walker's recommendation of his book led to much outrage, especially on social media. Feeling uncomfortable by the unexpected controversy, UUA officials reportedly rescinded the invitation to Walker before the contract was signed.

Almost immediately afterward they began discussing the possibility with Angela Davis, another iconic American woman, philosopher, and social activist. As with Walker, however, shortly before her contract was supposed to be signed, the Birmingham Civil Rights Institute rescinded an award it had given her in response to members of the local Jewish community in Birmingham who protested her support of the Boycott, Divestment, Sanctions (BDS) Movement against Israel, and her vocal support of Palestinian rights. According to my sources, UUA officials then decided it best to also rescind its invitation to Davis.

Sometime between when this occurred on January 7th, and January 12th, the date the 2019 Ware lecturer was scheduled to be announced to the GA Planning Committee, a deal was hastily made with Richard Blanco, whom the UUA announced with the following one sentence description: "Selected by President Obama as the fifth inaugural poet in US history, he is the youngest and the first Latino, immigrant, and gay person to serve in this role." Of all that could have been said of this distinguished presenter, it is telling that the UUA chose to emphasize attributes of his identity rather than the uniqueness of his work and quality of his character.

The rejection of Alice Walker and, perhaps more so, Angela Davis, is indicative of the greater problem with political correctness, at least as far as Unitarian Universalists should be concerned; the inability to tolerate hearing anything or anyone one disagrees with. We live in a society today where the definition of *tolerance* has been turned upside down, in which it is considered intolerant to say things others disagree with, rather than the unwillingness to listen to those with whom we disagree. Instead, some use PC to silence their unwanted voices, to demonize their persons with *ad hominem* attacks, and to disinvite and protest their very presence in this world, harkening back to the days of those doctrinal authorities Unitarians arose to resist, and to the Inquisitions, heresy trials, and witch-hunts that worked to suppress them.

8. Witch Hunts

It may be, having become disempowered within society at large and, thus, retreated into the cloistered realms of their own institutions, that liberals now obsess over what language ought to be used amongst themselves as a means of compensation. Feeling powerless to affect meaningful change in the world, some strive, instead, to gain control over those within their own organizations. "Whether one thinks of the Reign of Terror during the French Revolution, the Stalinist Show Trials, or the McCarthy period in the United States, the phenomenon is the same," sociologist Albert Bergesen once wrote, "a community becomes intensely mobilized to rid itself of internal enemies."[72]

Coddling metaphorically uses terms like "'Maoist,' 'McCarthyite,' Jacobian,' and above all, 'witch-hunt,'" to describe this phenomenon. "Those who apply such terms," they say, "are claiming that what we are witnessing… exemplifies a situation long studied by sociologists in which a community becomes obsessed with religious or ideological purity and believes it needs to find and punish enemies within its own ranks in order to hold itself together."[73]

An extremely disturbing example of this phenomenon, by my judgement, occurred during the 2017 LREDA (Liberal Religious Education Directors Association) Fall Conference in Denver, Colorado. Gregory Rouillard and Jared Finkelstein had been contracted to lead participants in two days of Nonviolent Communication (NVC) training. Rouillard and Finkelstein are both certified NVC trainers and professional facilitators, as well as cofounders of the Seven Principles Project, which works to

---

[72] Ibid., p. 101.
[73] Ibid., p. 99.

help communities of faith cultivate covenantal relationships based on Unitarian Universalist principles. They share many years of experience successfully presenting to religious organizations, including to UU groups, but nothing had prepared them for what seems fated to have occurred at the LREDA conference.

Little more than an hour into the first day's program, Rouillard says, "It became increasingly clear there was a small group of people who were not participating in the way we had invited them to." At some point one of those in this group began openly questioning what they were doing, claiming "NVC is manipulative, it's domination, it's created by a white man..." Rouillard pauses, unwilling to repeat some of what he remembers hearing, "...Anyway, lots of judgements about Marshall Rosenberg and so on." Though startled by accusations Rosenberg, who developed NVC based upon his personal experiences with anti-Semitism, was being characterized as a white supremacist, Rouillard and Finkelstein decided to "go with what was happening and give a voice to what was wanting to be said, and work with it to bring it into the context of what we were doing." But someone in the back of the conference room became increasingly agitated by their efforts to do so and became vocally critical of NVC.

"How dare you!" The person exclaimed.

"I don't know what to do," Finkelstein finally responded, "because I keep reflecting what I'm hearing and trying to understand what's important to you, but I don't get that you trust that I hear you. Do you have that trust?"

"No, I don't," the hostile attendee said.

"What can I do?" Finkelstein asked.

"Sit down and shut up!"

The perplexed facilitators did exactly that as attendees began debating amongst themselves, some of whom were confused by what they were witnessing. "What's going on? We were having a great time. We were learning. We were having fun. We were interacting," Rouillard recalls some of them saying. After about 20 minutes, LREDA's President at the time, Annie Scott entered and reportedly said, "We're done here," then segregated the whites from the persons of color. A room was then set up down the hall where the persons of color were invited to visit with the LREDA Diversity and Inclusion Team to discuss what had happened. This bias toward those representing only one identity group may explain the discrepancy between Scott, who later claimed, "some people of color challenged them, as did some white people and others with marginalized identities,"[74] and Rouillard's recollection that they were "mostly white people." More troubling, however, is that Scott's letter of explanation (November 8th, 2017) defamatorily referred to the two men as "speakers... that embodied white supremacy and patriarchy."

Beyond this Rouillard admits, "I don't recollect a lot of the details because at this point, I was kind of in shock. I had never in a decade of professional facilitation been treated this way, or ever encountered a situation that wasn't manageable." A short time later he and Finkelstein were asked to leave the conference. Until my interviews with them, nearly two years later, both men say not a single

---

[74] From Annie Scott's "Post Fall Conference Message form the Board," Issued to the LREDA Membership, November 8th, 2017.

person from the UUA had ever reached out to check on them or query about the incident. This is so even though Rouillard, who has himself been an active Unitarian Universalist for decades, had considered several attending the conference his close friends. One anonymous UU minister later suggested, "That's because they are afraid of being banished—made the enemy—because they're your friends."

Rouillard says he was also informed the entire ruckus had been part of a setup, "'This is not an accident. This was preplanned,'" he was told. "'There was a lot of stuff on social media organizing this disruptive action, and that it was organized and planned.' So there really was nothing we could do." Although he acknowledges he has no proof of this, such proof, it turns out, does exist. Immediately following the disastrous conference, another LREDA staff member issued a formal statement to its membership explicitly stating;

> Recently, on Facebook, we posted a marketing piece for Fall Conference. The ad contained photos of two key conference presenters, both of whom are white and male. We heard concerns from some of you, questioning how this came to be; wondering, in light of the events of this past year—the teach-ins, the focus on dismantling white supremacy in our UU culture, and the institutional commitments to make changes to systems in our denomination—how did we end up here?

Rouillard verifies this same staff member had contacted him in advance of the conference expressing concern about these posts, asking, "Is there some NVC trainer who is a woman or a woman of color?" Rouillard said, "yes," and offered to help contact her. His impulse in that moment told him, "This is too risky. Let's back out," but by the end of their conversation the staffer said, "No, I feel confident about it. I think you guys will be fine."

These preconference communications prove beyond doubt that some were upset before Rouillard and Finkelstein ever spoke a word, not because of anything they could have said, since they hadn't yet said anything, but simply because they are "white and male," and, for this reason alone, as Scott's letter of explanation explicitly concludes, they "embodied white supremacy and patriarchy."

This also explains the confusion some in attendance expressed regarding what they were witnessing. As one participant, new to LREDA at the time, anonymously told me, the reasons given for such a tremendous show of disrespect and anger at the facilitators "was hard to understand." They were criticized for forcing intimacy when leading the group in an exercise requiring them to look silently into the eyes of another attendee. They were accused of being patronizing for coming off the speaker's platform in order to be on the same level as everyone else. They were accused of being racist for asking participants to please arrive to their sessions on time.

Once more, I will leave to you to determine if catastrophizing the behavior of these men was warranted. My intention here is only to point out Gregory Rouillard and Jared Finkelstein likely did nothing worthy of such disrespect and indignity, and, likewise, could have done nothing to prevent it. Theirs was an original sin, the congenital condition of having been born both "white and male." This alone was enough for those who came with an apparent agenda to disrupt Rouillard and Finkelstein's efforts and cause, as *Coddling* puts it, "a surprising, 'out of nowhere' eruption of 'mass groupthink' in which trivial things are taken as grave attacks on a vulnerable community."[75]

"The immediate impact on me was devastating personally and professionally," Rouillard says. It took him a while, but he was able to regain his confidence upon returning to work the following spring. "'Oh, okay, I can still do this,'" the work reassured him, "'There's nothing wrong with me.' And I really recognized this was an expression of something within the UUA culture, it wasn't about me at all." Today Rouillard says he's more fulfilled in both his life and work than ever, though he has not worked with Unitarian Universalists since the LREDA incident.

Finkelstein admits, "It's awful to fight with the people you are the most similar with. It's an awful feeling to be talking to the people you imagine are your family, and your friends, and of like-mindedness, and just being told you're racist and you're condescending." Yet he also maintains much compassion for everyone present at the LREDA event and believes their motivations were good. He just hopes the UUA in general finds better ways to bring people together to honestly discuss the many difficulties around the vital work of anti-oppression, or, as he likes to call it, *beloved community*. "At the end of the day," he says, "Gregory and I were doing the best that we could, having been invited to preach our message of love the way we understand the expression of love and conflict resolution in the world."

---

[75] Lukianoff & Haidt, ibid., p. 106.

In light of all that *Coddling* addresses is going on in the U.S., such an event happening within the UUA and its emerging PC culture could have been predicted. Citing the work of Columbia University linguist John McWhorter, Lukianoff and Haidt point out "the term 'white supremacist' is now used in an 'utterly athletic, recreational way,' as a 'battering ram' to attack anyone who departs from the party line."[76] Regarding the LREDA incident, however, Rouillard and Finkelstein had said nothing contrary to the party line. As Rouillard says, "It's ironic that we were labeled as embodying racism and patriarchy. We were there to offer an opportunity to learn together and create a new system that works for everyone." Their supposed offence, rather, as has been firmly established, was being "white and male," the "embodiment of white supremacy and patriarchy," and for this reason alone, some believe, should not have been allowed to have a presence at the event, nor even have their offensive images presented in its promotional materials.

Sociologist Eduardo Bonilla-Silva points out this is precisely the problem with too broad a definition of *racism*; "Racism, which is or can be almost everything, is proven by anything done (or not done) by whites. The analyst identifies the existence of racism because any action done by whites is labeled as racist."[77]

Fortunately, upon contacting the UUA's Communications department, I have been assured there is, "without equivocation," no policy in place prohibiting the images of persons who are "white and male" from being

---

[76] Ibid., p. 86.
[77] Bonilla-Silva, Eduardo, *White Supremacy & Racism in the Post-Civil Rights Era*, Lynne Rienner Publishers, Boulder, CO, 2001, p. 27f.

printed in the organization's publications or on its website. With its almost singular emphasis on antiracism and anti-oppression work, however, it is reasonable they will include a preponderance of persons who are not white and male. This may also explain why a person who is "white and male" has not been invited to offer the prestigious Ware Lecture at the UUA's General Assembly since 2002, or, increasingly, to fill any prominent speaking opportunities at UUA meetings and gatherings.

Anecdotally speaking, however, it doesn't explain a peculiar and troubling experience of my own as a member of the 2017 GA Worship Arts team during which its Chair told me, "Your service is the whitest of them all. What can we do about it?" I was responsible for putting together a morning worship service that included three persons of color, two women who are white, four of whom I was instructed to include, and one local minister who was, indeed, "white and male," whom I can only presume was the real concern. After beginning my response by listing the races and ethnicities of my participants, I interrupted myself, saying, "I'm sorry, I just don't feel comfortable talking about people in these terms." At that point the conversation was dropped.

Nor does it explain an April 2018 retweet from Leslie Mac, the Board Chair of BLUU (Black Lives of UU Organizing Collective). Originally composed by an individual who was soon to be ordained into Unitarian Universalist ministry, the tweet stated, "Throw away all those white liberals. For real for real. They [are] all garbage with limited understanding of their culpability of harming marginalized people with their white savior behavior and ill conceived notions about what other ppl need to do."

After raising concerns about the tweet with two UUA Board members, I received a brief email from one of them stating:

> I shared your concern about the tweet with other board members. One board member indicated that he had seen it blow up on Facebook. He said that it was taken out of context. Specifically, he said that the folks complaining about the post never went and looked at the actual link referenced—which was to a pretty gross article about some actor saying how poor people should use food stamps better. That was what Leslie was referring to according to him.

Here, too, I will leave it up to my reader to determine if this explanation, and the Board's quick dismissal of it, is satisfactory.[78] I will only point out the tremendous contrast between the "principle of charity" extended to one who overtly refers to a whole group of people as "garbage" we should "throw away," and the treatment Rouillard and Finkelstein received, who said nothing of the sort although their every word and action were met as uncharitably as imaginable.

A similar experience happened in response to Rev. Dr. Andy Burnette, the "white and male" minister who, in 2017, had initially been offered the UUA's Southern Regional Lead, a position he ended up declining after the decision to hire him led to accusations of white supremacy. When he mentioned the related stress had exacerbated health issues for some of his family members while chatting on a

---

[78] The Wall Street Journal opinion article the tweet refers to can be found at http://t.co/uT94u5V0A8.

UU ministers social media platform, he was told, "Victimhood does not look good on you." He was also informed, "Telling your story is centering whiteness. You need to not tell your story so they can decenter whiteness." After sharing some of his pain with his congregation, Rev. Burnette recounts, "An 80-year-old African American woman member put her arm around me and told me, 'Now you know what it's like to be tokenized. All they see is your whiteness.' I lost a lot of faith in UUism around that."

It is my belief all that has been mentioned in this section has emerged because the UUA, like other liberal institutions, has become engrossed in the ethics of identity, having largely abandoned our humanistic tradition, the recognition of our common humanity, in the process. This has not only led to the dehumanization of the denomination's "white and male" members, ministers, and guests by some who consider them mere symbols of "white supremacy and patriarchy," but also to the tokenization of its nonwhite-male members, ministers, and guests whose images and, therefore, bodies are being harnessed in its publications and upon its platforms to portray the denomination as being far more diverse than it actually is.

Hitler is often called the "embodiment of evil," not because he had a human body and others with human bodies had done evil things, but because of the inhuman evils he himself committed. Unitarian Universalists, who profess to respect the worth and dignity of every person, should already know that excluding, prejudging, or stereotyping anyone simply because they bear certain arbitrary genetic qualities is morally wrong.[79] So is the underdeveloped punitive mindset of retributive, fair-is-fair, even-Steven, justice that leads some to lash out at those individuals whom they have reduced to mere symbols. Each one of us is far more than a symbol, far more than the identities we choose to take on, or those that have been forced upon us. Each of us is also part of one human family, whether or not we recognize it about ourselves, or whether or not others recognize it about us. This doesn't mean some of us, whole groups of us, have not and are not suffering more than others, especially many who are not "white and male," in what remains a systemically white supremacist country.

What it does mean is that we are more when we are together than when we are apart. We are stronger and more powerful and more whole when we are able to support one another, and love one another, and see one another for all that we are. That's what the root of the word *respect* means,

---

[79] Erich Fromm helps us grasp how something like this might occur. In his book about how we become fascist, *Escape From Freedom*, Fromm distinguishes between what he calls the *rebel* and the *revolutionary*. The *rebel* is someone who feels powerless and is fighting to become powerful, whereas the true *revolutionary* is fighting to change society for the good of all. The *rebel* is selfish; the *revolutionary* is altruistic. The *rebel* is an authoritarian character; the *revolutionary* is a genuine liberator. These distinctions are important because *rebels* and *revolutionaries* are often fighting side-by-side in the same cause. The only way to tell them apart is by their methodology. The revolutionary cares for everyone involved in the struggle: friend or foe. "A rebel" Fromm says, "is one who wants to overthrow authority because of his resentment and, as a result, to make himself the authority in place of the one he has overthrown. And very often, at the very moment when he reaches his aim, he makes friends with the very authority he was fighting so bitterly before." [Fromm, Erich, *Escape from Freedom*, Avon Books, The Heart Corporation, New York, NY, 1941, 1966, p. 140.]

"to be seen." If, however, UUA culture now considers it appropriate to exclude persons who are "white and male" from being seen and heard because they are the "embodiment of white supremacy and patriarchy," I hope the organization will be transparent about this "institutional change," so those who may fundamentally differ with this approach can offer their dissent or, at least, decide if they wish to remain a part of it.

9. Gray Areas

It becomes difficult to recognize the error in our own thinking within the echo chamber of political correctness. Those held inside its comforting embrace hear only their own reassuring opinions repeated back to themselves. Those ensnared within its unforgiving grip are too frightened to disagree, afraid of being crushed and "thrown away" like "garbage." *Coddling* suggests this unwillingness to think critically about one's own opinions is the result of *Emotional Reasoning*, which it likens to riding atop an elephant:

> Emotional reasoning is the cognitive distortion that occurs whenever the rider interprets what is happening in ways that are consistent with the elephant's reactive emotional state, without investigating what is true. The rider then acts like a lawyer or press secretary whose job is to rationalize and justify the elephant's pre-ordained conclusions, rather than to inquire into—or even be curious about—what is really true.[80]

---

[80] Lukianoff and Haidt, ibid., p. 35.

The protected politically correct status quo then feels completely justified in dehumanizing and demonizing others in the name of not offending anyone, protecting others from harm, and establishing greater tolerance. Sociologist James Davidson Hunter says this is what happens when:

> A position is so "obviously superior," so "obviously correct," and its opposite is so "obviously out of bounds" that they are beyond discussion and debate. Indeed, to hold the "wrong" opinion, one must be either mentally imbalanced (phobic—as in *homophobic*, irrational, codependent, or similarly afflicted) or, more likely, evil.[81]

The way beyond the emotionally driven thinking the evidence presented in this article suggests is becoming rampant within the Unitarian Universalist Association is to make use of the principles and skills that have, until know, been at the heart of our religion—welcoming and encouraging genuine dissent and dialogue; remaining openminded, openhearted, and respectful toward others; and questioning and examining our own assumptions. In this case, in particular, it may be helpful to examine exactly what we mean, and what we ought to mean, by multiculturalism, equality, and identity. Here I shall begin to close this essay with the hope of beginning the conversation.

Multiculturalism not Segregation

Unitarian Universalism has long emphasized the importance of diversity and multiculturalism, as it should, providing

---

[81] Devine, ibid., p. 28.

these terms mean what they suggest, establishing a society based upon our commitment to the worth and dignity of every person, "in which," as Francis Fukuyama puts it, "recognition is due not just to a narrow class of people, but to everyone."[82] Yet it should be remembered the idea of diversity was also once offered by social conservatives as an alternative to such pluralism. As Philip Devine says, "Diversity, though currently celebrated on the Left, is a traditionally conservative idea, usually opposed to equality."[83]

In his book, *Democracy on Trial*, Jean Bethke Elshtain further explains, "It seems best, according to this conservative argument, to allow natural differences—seen as inequalities—to work themselves out, even if the result is a stratified inegalitarian society in the social and economic sense even as we remain equal only before the law."[84] As recent as 1993, one of those respected conservative thinkers, George Kennan, the U.S. Ambassador to the Soviet Union during the Eisenhower Administration, wrote the following:

> Forced segregation? Of course not. But neither should there be forced desegregation. People should be allowed to do what comes naturally. There are a great many instances in which people prefer the proximity, the neighborhood, and the social intimacy of people who share their customs, their way of talking, their way of looking at things...[85]

---

[82] Fukuyama, ibid., p. 37.
[83] Devine, ibid., p. 100.
[84] Elshtain, Jean Bethke, *Democracy on Trial*, Basic Books, New York, NY, 1995, p. 69.
[85] Kennan, George F., *Around the Cragged Hill*, W.W. Norton & Company, New York, NY, 1993, p. 127.

Since it has become socially unacceptable to promote a "separate but equal" society, as it ought to be, Kennan's line of reasoning illustrates what Eduardo Bonilla-Silva means by *color-blind racism*. Referring to this particular frame as the "naturalization of matters," one of the four dominant frames he's identified, Bonilla-Silva provides the following example: "Neighborhood segregation is a *sad* but *natural* thing since people want to live with people who are like them."[86] Kennan goes on to say:

> I have lived in and read about cities in other countries where several cultural and ethnic communities lived peacefully side by side, each in its own part of town, its members mingling, to be sure, with others in the premises and functions of employment, but looking to their own particular communities for the meeting of their social, religious, and educational needs... Each of these communities had, in this instance, its own schools, newspapers, clubs, theaters, and diversions. So long as they viewed each other with tolerance, and so long as any one of them did not attempt to lord it over the others ...all went well... No melting pot was thought necessary, and indeed, none was ever achieved.[87]

Here Kennan extends the *naturalization of matters* framework to suggest a segregated society can get along just fine. So long as we tolerate each identity group's differences, everyone is happy being with "their own kind."

---

[86] Bonilla-Silva, ibid., p. 141.
[87] Kennan, ibid., p. 128.

But multiculturalism and diversity are meant to bring us together as members of one pluralistic society, recognizing we are alike in our common humanity, allowing us to embrace our differences even while fully embracing each other. Like color-blind racism, however, these concepts can also be used by liberal identitarians to morally justify the belief we are so different we cannot be together, nor even be allowed to influence each other in our separate but equal cultures. To be inspired enough to adopt the ways of those who are different, especially those society has traditionally exploited or oppressed, is now disparaged as "misappropriation," even though, as Devine says, "To accept a tradition is also to identify with the community whose tradition it is."[88] It is not possible to truly appreciate and accept each other without also influencing each other's ways and beliefs. Just as we cannot prevent communicating illnesses, or exchanging genetic material to reproduce whole new persons, regardless of our differing identities, we cannot help but communicate, contract, and exchange culture because it is all human culture. We are one species, one human family whether or not we recognize it about ourselves, or others recognize it about us.

Yet, it is in the name of multiculturalism the UUA now regularly divides its members into caucuses based purely upon narrow identity-based categories—ethnicity, gender, sexuality, etc., etc. Or by providing "healing rooms" at our assemblies into which nonwhites can escape from injurious microaggressions committed by whites who are forbidden to enter. Or by vilifying those who dare speak, even supportively, on behalf of those outside their own

---

[88] Devine, ibid., p. 9.

assigned identity group. The goal of multiculturalism and diversity, rather, should be about bringing us together, as one unified community that appreciates, shares, and celebrates our differences, recognizing, "Each individual in the contemporary world is a nexus of many different cultural identities, a fact that resists assimilation into a multicultural framework."[89]

Equality and Freedom

At the outset it may seem equality and freedom go hand in hand, but in practice they are often at great odds, like the poles at two ends of a spectrum. Today, for example, "the dogma of radical economic individualism that Reaganism normalized" has resulted in extreme income inequality, in which very few have far more wealth than most everyone else. This is what happens when individuals and groups of individuals are completely free to pursue their own interests without regard for how their freedoms impact the wellbeing of others. It's an example of how an overemphasis upon freedom (i.e., freedom from taxes, freedom from regulations, freedom from government), accompanied by little regard for social responsibility, can result in extreme inequality in many areas.

On the other end of the spectrum, an extreme emphasis on equality can result in societies that are unbearably oppressive. We need only look back to when the Social Democratic Labor Party seized power in Russia in 1917. The Bolshevik ("majority") Revolution involved scores of mostly young people under age 30 eager to

---

[89] Ibid., p. 50.

establish income equality for ordinary working people. When their Party leader, Vladimir Lenin, took control of the newly established Soviet ("workers committee") Union in 1922, he promised enough "bread, land, and peace"[90] for everyone, though an estimated six-million people had already starved to death as a result of the five-year revolution.

The well-intended revolution, grounded in the youth of the nation's demand for equality, resulted in one of the most oppressive governments in modern history. The overbearing State they erected enforced equality upon its citizens by tightly restricting individual freedom and felt morally justified in doing so. In order to prevent the greed and selfishness fostered by capitalist societies, which they believed lead to egregious inequalities, the Communist State sought to suppress these individualistic urges by strictly controlling every aspect of their people's lives—where they lived, where they worked, how much they earned, how they dressed, their education, and, above all, what they thought and were allowed to say.

While visiting Eastern Europe today, one is sure to notice how colorful many of the buildings have become since the collapse of Communism. This is so because people weren't allowed to paint their homes during Communism. All the homes had to look alike, covered only with drab gray stucco or unpainted concrete. The same is true of the colossal concrete Communist housing units in larger cities, which are increasingly being painted with bright bands of yellows, greens, blues, and pinks. During Communism, equality

---

[90] Newman, Michael, *Socialism: A Very Short Introduction,* Oxford University Press, 2005, (Kindle) Loc. 702.

meant everyone had to be the same. Painted homes, colorful clothes, and, above all, speaking of things forbidden by the State, made people stand out too much as individuals. Individual freedom couldn't coexist with its puritanical notion of equality. As Ambassador Kennan observed, "The main thing was that no one should live better than anyone else. Uniformity was an end in itself."[91]

This is why Fukuyama calls "the twin principles of freedom and democracy... the moral core of modern liberal democracy."[92] In the U.S. freedom without equality once resulted in the horror of slavery, the segregation of Jim Crow, violent voter suppression and terrorism against blacks, and, to this day, a massive incarceration program designed to disenfranchise nonwhite voters, amongst many other injustices and inequalities. Perhaps some feel this extreme situation requires an extreme course correction by swinging in the opposite direction, eliminating the ideologies responsible for these cruelties and inequities by utterly suppressing their expression. But, as we have seen, equality without freedom only results in making everyone equally miserable.

In 1956, social psychologist Erich Fromm complained, "Equality today means 'sameness,' rather than oneness."[93] Understanding the difference can make all the difference in establishing a balance between these two essential social needs. The kind of equality the emerging culture of safetyism, identitarianism, and political

---

[91] Kennan, ibid., p. 121.
[92] Fukuyama, ibid., p. 46.
[93] Fromm, Erich, *The Art of Loving*, (Harper & Row, New York, NY, 1956), 12.

correctness seeks to enforce, which now has a foothold in the UUA, misunderstands equality to mean "sameness."

Until now, however, Unitarian Universalism has understood equality to mean "oneness," based upon our humanistic tradition and its belief in the common humanity of all persons. Yet, today, as Fukuyama makes clear, "The rise of identity politics in modern liberal democracies is one of the chief threats they face, and unless we can work our way back to more universal understandings of human dignity, we will doom ourselves to continuing conflict."[94] If he is correct, and our tiny denomination, which today has less than 200,000 members, less than .05 percent of the American population, then we must return to those principles that pull us together and quickly abandon those mentioned that are driving us apart and can only end in our ruin.

Common Enemy Identity vs. Common Humanity Identity

While appearing on the October 12, 2018 episode of *Real Time with Bill Maher*, during a discussion on the subject, Eddie Glaude Jr., Professor of Religion and African American Studies at Princeton University, said political correctness means "white straight men can't walk around saying whatever the hell is on their minds." Although a peculiar definition within the context of the conversation, I fully agree with Glaude; PC, along with safetyism and identity liberalism, is about suppressing freedom of speech, not only for those it concludes are the "embodiment of white supremacy and patriarchy," but of anyone who violates its

---

[94] Fukuyama, ibid., p. xvi.

unforgiving expectations. It doesn't allow honest or open discussion of ideological differences. Instead, any ideas its adherents disagree with are immediately judged injurious and harmful, and those who utter them are shamed, dehumanized, or demonized.

Lukianoff and Haidt tell us this mindset is based upon what they call, "The Untruth of Us vs. Them: *Life is a battle between good people and bad people.*"[95] On the one hand, this untruth, that people are purely evil because of the ideas in their heads, or because of some arbitrary congenital physical qualities, can feel extremely intoxicating because it helps individuals achieve the human need for belonging by bonding with others who feel the same way. On the other hand, it can lead to the kind of groupthink that is often unsubstantiated by reason or empirical reality. "When the 'tribal switch' is activated," *Coddling* explains, "we bind ourselves more tightly to the group, we embrace and defend the group's moral matrix, and we stop thinking for ourselves."[96] It is also true, they continue, "Conditions of peace and prosperity, by contrast, generally turn down tribalism,"[97] which is why, as we continue to address the injustices against members associated with specific groups, we must also emphasize our common humanity, that, as Chief Joseph of the Nez Perce once said, "The Earth is the Mother of all people, and all people should have equal rights upon it..."[98]

---

[95] Lukianoff & Haidt, ibid., p. 4.
[96] Ibid., p. 58.
[97] Ibid., p. 59.
[98] Freedman, Russell, *Indian Chiefs*, Scholastic Inc., New York, NY, 1987, p. 111.

Coddling further distinguishes between two kinds of identity politics, *Common-Enemy* and *Common-Humanity*. The first of these, as you will have guessed, is based upon the Untruth of Us vs. Them, some of the manifestations of which I have presented throughout this essay. It is worth directly noting, in light of such evidence, that Lukianoff and Haidt specifically state that for those who consider *life a battle between good people and evil people*, "The main axes of oppression usually point to one intersectional address: straight white males."[99]

Common-Humanity Identity Politics, on the other hand is epitomized, they say, by the philosophy of Dr. Martin Luther King, Jr.:

> Part of Dr. King's genius was that he appealed to the shared morals and identities of Americans by using the unifying languages of religion and patriotism. He repeatedly used the metaphor of family, referring to people of all races and religions as "brothers" and "sisters." He spoke often of the need for love and forgiveness, harkening back to the words of Jesus and echoing ancient wisdom from many cultures: "Love is the only force capable of transforming an enemy into a friend" and "Darkness cannot drive out darkness; only light can do that. Hate cannot drive out hate; only love can do that."[100]

As the cover page of the edition of the *UU World* discussed earlier ironically states, "Nothing We Do Will Be Perfect." Like the other polarities I've mentioned in this

---

[99] Lukianoff & Haidt, ibid., p. 70.
[100] Ibid., p. 60.

section, finding the balance between *Common-Enemy Identity Politics* and *Common-Humanity Identity Politics* is not easy, nor is their nebulous demarcation easy to distinguish. So, instead of demanding puritanical perfection, which is the goal of PC, safetyism, and identitarianism, we can only keep these distinctions in mind and do our best; hoping, as we have a right to expect among Unitarian Universalists, the principle of charity will be liberally extended to all.

> Identity can be mobilized in ways that emphasize an overarching common humanity while making the case that some *fellow human beings* are denied dignity and rights because they belong to a particular group, or it can be mobilized in ways that amplify our ancient tribalism and bind people together in shared hatred of a *group* that serves as the unifying common enemy.[101]

Fortunately, Unitarian Universalism need only recall its roots to embrace an ethic based upon our common humanity. Even so, at this crossroads in our history, it has become a choice we must make. Will we abandon this principle as part of the "institutional change" our denominational leaders are now initiating, replacing it with the divisive philosophies of safetyism, identitarianism, and political correctness, or will we wholly embrace it that we might wholly embrace each other? Will we listen to the voices of our ancestors calling us forward, or, even while claiming not to believe in Hell, pave our way there with good intentions?

---

[101] Ibid.

I WANT A DIVORCE

A Case for Splitting the Unitarian Universalist Association

1. The Merger

Until now, there have been two major conflicts within Unitarianism: the *Transcendentalist Controversy* and the *Humanist Debate* (alt. *Humanist-Theist Controversy*). The first of these, which began in the 1830s, resulted in a shift away from traditional Christian language and beliefs (i.e., Biblical authority, supernaturalism, the existence of a personal deity), and toward naturalism (the idea everything emerges from natural causes) to define itself. The second, the Humanist Debate, which began nearly a century later, resulted in the denomination becoming far less sectarian and its inclusion of some members who rejected theism altogether. Today, not quite a century later, though few yet recognize it, we are experiencing the third major conflict in our history, a denominational *Identity Crisis*, which, I shall argue, is a culminating consequence of the merger of the

American Unitarian Association (AUA) and the Universalist Church of America in 1961.

Long before the formation of the Unitarian Universalist Association, many had recognized how much the two denominations shared in common and some envisioned a time when they might join together. Thomas Starr King (1824 – 1864), who considered himself both a Universalist and a Unitarian, famously quipped, "The Universalist... believe that God is too good to damn us forever: and you Unitarians believe you are too good to be damned."[102] It was as early as 1865, during the very first meeting of the National Conference of Unitarian Churches, that a merger of the two faiths was officially discussed, leading to the establishment of a committee to explore the possibility. But it wasn't until the late 1930s, when Frederick May Eliot became President of the American Unitarian Association (1937–1958), that a serious effort to unite the two faiths began. It was about this same time the Association's Commission on Appraisal issued a report recommending, "Unitarians should free themselves from the sectarian spirit by cooperating more fully with other denominations, by taking part in the growing movement of the Free Church Fellowship, and by entering wholeheartedly into the worldwide fellowship of religious liberals in many lands."[103] The Free Church Fellowship, formed by AUA President Louis Craig Cornish, who served just prior to Eliot

---

[102] Frothingham, Richard, *A Tribute to Starr King*, Ticknor and Fields, Boston, MA, 1865, p. 121.
[103] *The Report of the Commission on Appraisal for the American Unitarian Association*, "Unitarians Face a New Age," 25 Beacon Street, Boston, MA, 1936.

in the 1930s, was created for the purpose of establishing an international organization of liberal faiths. "Although it hoped to attract liberals from all over Protestantism, its essential support was for the Unitarians and Universalists."[104]

Though the Free Church Fellowship didn't last long, its hope for a merger continued. Eliot often spoke publicly of his support for unifying the Unitarians and Universalists and, in 1953, the establishment of the Council of Liberal Churches "merged the administrative functions of the religious education, publications, and public relations of the two denominations,"[105] which put the process of merger well underway. Soon a joint commission on merger was established and, in 1959, a biennial conference of Unitarians and Universalists took place in Syracuse, New York, during which the merger was agreed upon by representatives of both denominations—an agreement that was finalized in 1961 with the formal establishment of the Unitarian Universalist Association.

2. Similarities & Differences

There was, indeed, much the Unitarians and the Universalists long shared in common that made such a merger seem workable to many. Both were at odds with Calvinism and evangelical Protestantism (as expressed in the Great Awakening and Second Birth movements). Both held

---

[104] Robinson, David, *The Unitarians and the Universalists*, Greenwood Press, Westport, CT, 1985, p. 173.
[105] Ibid.

views of a benevolent God and rejected notions of human depravity. Early in the 1800s, some referred to Unitarians as "Universalists in disguise," and Universalists as "indistinguishable from Unitarians."[106] Yet, as historian David Robinson points out, "That the union had been discussed for more than a century before it was completed is perhaps the most convincing testimony to the difficulties inherent in it."[107]

The major differences between the two liberal faiths centered around theology and class. Since its inception, for instance, Universalism had been at odds with the religious establishment. This was so from the time its founder John Murray was publicly pushed, kicked, and stoned for preaching against Hell. Later, when his congregation in Gloucester, Massachusetts, the Independent Christian Church (the first Universalist society in America, est. 1779) refused to pay its required taxes in support of the officially sanctioned First Parrish Church, their belongings were confiscated by the authorities as recompense. In short, from its very beginning, Universalism was the faith of outsiders who identified themselves as such.

Unitarian congregations, by contrast, were among those, like First Parrish Church, considered orthodox and were, thus, legally supported by public taxes. These "Standing Order" churches, as they were called, were among those whose clergy had agreed upon a certain set of beliefs. Since such "standing" included public funding, Unitarians were part of an intellectually (and generally better educated)

---

[106] Miller, Russell E., *The Larger Hope: The First Century of the Universalist Church in America 1770-1870*, Unitarian Universalist Association, Boston, MA, 1979, p. 795.
[107] Robinson, ibid., p. 168f.

elite group with special privileges. Henry Bellows, the Unitarian minister who founded the National Conference of Unitarian Churches in 1865 and was one of the strongest proponents of merger, considered this "difference in social class as the greatest barrier to that unity."[108]

Theologically the Unitarians tended toward Enlightenment thinking and, thus, filtered their beliefs through science and reason. This led to the abandonment of supernaturalism, including a disbelief in Biblical miracles and a rejection of theism (belief in a personal god). Though at odds with established Christianity, the Universalists were, ironically, more theologically orthodox than the Unitarians. As Robinson puts it, "Neither the movement away from a scriptural basis of faith nor the abandonment of a faith in Jesus made as much headway within Universalism as within Unitarianism. In a sense this is to say that Universalism remained more conservative, but it might be more accurate to say that Universalists continued to draw liberal conclusions from their traditional bases of faith."[109]

These differences, which may now appear minor, were enough to cause some opposition to the merger. Unitarians, who had increasingly abandoned orthodox Christian thinking and rejected any notion of a centralized religious authority, spurned the possibility of becoming sectarian by joining with a religious sect. Universalists, on the other hand, retained their belief in the Bible and their faith in Jesus, and worried about joining with a group that did not, as well as being concerned about losing their heretical identity. Although such opposition wasn't enough

---

[108] Ibid., p. 169.
[109] Ibid., p. 171.

to prevent the merger, that these issues remained unresolved proved itself true before the final agreement's ink had dried.

Regarding the new Association's draft Constitution, accepted during the 1959 Syracuse joint meeting, there was much prior debate over the Universalists' wish to insert, "To cherish and spread the universal truths of Jesus," and, "Judeo-Christian tradition," into the document's stated purposes. In response to Unitarian objections, many of whom no longer considered themselves part of Protestant Christianity, the Universalists agreed to delete any reference to Jesus if they could still refer to "our Judeo-Christian heritage." The Unitarians agreed only after the word "our" was substituted with "the." "But this slight variation in wording," Robinson points out, "and the importance attached to it by the delegates, indicated the problems not yet resolved by the Unitarians and the Universalists."[110]

Hence, as Russell Miller makes clear in his monumental history on Universalism, *The Larger Hope*, although some historians have retrospectively made them seem almost interchangeable, "the temptation to anticipate the twentieth century union of the two denominations, which did take place must be strongly resisted;"

> The ostensible similarities of the two groups as "twin heresies" in the nineteenth century, noted by not only those within both denominations but by many outside observers, actually concealed deep differences of theology, class configuration, philosophy, behavior, and

---

[110] Ibid., p. 174.

attitudes which cannot be easily overlooked or minimized.[111]

After more than a century of considering such a merger, however, by the time it finally happened the Unitarians and Universalists had evolved to share one important point in common—their commitment to the establishment of a universal religion of humanity. It was for this reason Rev. Henry Bellows soon changed the name of the First Congregational (Unitarian) Church in New York City, after becoming its minister in 1839, to All Souls Church. More importantly, it's why he worked to found the National Conference of Unitarian Churches in 1859, in order to include entire churches into Unitarian membership. Prior to this, the American Unitarian Association had only allowed individuals into its membership. Despite this expression of Unitarianism's general disdain for sectarian associations, however, Bellows felt the National Conference was a first step in advancing toward the greater goal of a universal religion of humanity. Robinson further reminds us the "confirmation of a universal religious sense in humanity," expressed by Unitarians as notable as Lydia Maria Child, James Freeman Clarke, and Samuel Johnson, also "helped to advance the notion of a universal liberal religion embodied in a universal nonsectarian church."[112]

Likewise, during the Centennial celebration of Universalism in 1870, denominational leaders began finally

---

[111] Miller, Russell E., *The Larger Hope: The First Century of the Universalist Church in America 1770-1870*, Unitarian Universalist Association, Boston, MA, 1979, p. 794.

[112] Robinson, ibid., p. 169.

shifting away from its Christian heritage to reimagine Universalism becoming a universal world religion, an attitude historian George H. Williams says "would become the dominant strand in the denomination."[113] With this, Church History professor Earnest Cassara writes, "A new type of Universalism is proclaimed which shifts the emphasis on universal from salvation to religion and describes Universalism as boundless in scope, as broad as humanity, and as infinite as the universe."[114]

If such a vision was ever to come true, it had to begin somewhere, and many believed there was nowhere better than among the two liberal religions that wanted it most. It was, thus, this joint desire to establish a universal religion of humanity that eventually made it possible for the Unitarians and Universalists to merge together after more than a century of flirting with the idea.

3. Our Identity Crisis

In his treatment of the merger in *The Unitarians and the Universalists*, Robinson further reminds us, "Consolidation is an act aimed at the future; there can be no consolidation of the past."[115] If this is so, it means the social and theological differences existing between Unitarians and Universalists prior to the merger have remained largely unaddressed, and are, perhaps, still festering within the UUA. It also means both traditions have become severed from the historical roots

---

[113] Williams, George H., "American Universalism: A Bicentennial Historical Essay," The Universalist Historical Society, Raleigh, North Carolina, 1971, p. 82.
[114] Robinson, ibid., p. 171.
[115] Ibid., p. 168.

that once held and guided their unique identities. And this means that together its members now have a nebulous understanding of who they are and what they're about. It means, to borrow a term coined by psychologist Erick Erickson in 1950, Unitarian Universalism has an *identity crisis*.

Though Erickson initially used this phrase in reference to the confusion some individual adolescents experience on their way to adulthood, he understood it could also be appropriately attributed to industries, associations, even entire nations. Hence, in addition to defining it as the "disorientation and role confusion occurring especially in adolescents," the Online Free Dictionary calls it, "An analogous state of confusion occurring in a social structure, such as an institution or a corporation."[116] Webster's Dictionary similarly says it can be "a state of confusion in an institution or organization regarding its nature or direction."[117]

Our common quest for the elusive "elevator speech" to explain what Unitarian Universalism means is but one symptom of our own organization's identity crisis. After more than five decades since the merger, many Unitarian Universalists still don't know how to adequately describe their religion to themselves, let alone to others. Some find it with so little meaning of its own that they feel compelled to add other traditions to the mix, describing themselves as Buddhist UUs, Christian UUs, Pagan UUs, Humanist UUs, etc., etc. Such descriptions would have been both unnecessary and inconceivable prior to the merger, at least

[116] http://www.thefreedictionary.com/identity+crisis
[117] http://www.merriam-webster.com/dictionary/identity%20crisis

69

not any less than it would be today to call oneself a "Buddhist Pentecostal," or a "Pagan Baptist." Before then, Unitarians knew who they were and what their faith tradition was about, as did Universalists, even amidst the conflicts that sometimes arose during their respective evolutionary histories.

This jumbled, if not relativistic, understanding of what Unitarian Universalism means to UUs themselves becomes apparent in a 2005 Commission on Appraisal report entitled, *Engaging our Theological Diversity*, asking UU members, "What holds us together?" One participant said, "It's the support network."[118] Another saw "the UU movement as an interreligious dialogue."[119] Another said UU congregations are comprised of "people who didn't fit in"[120] anywhere else. Still others actually complained about us not having a common belief. "This is where the UUA falls down," they said, "and why you have CUUPS and the Buddhists and the Christians and all these little subgroups— because we offer the hope of a spiritual journey, and we offer no tools to do it with."[121]

Many in the study placed the blame for this predicament on our theological diversity. As one participant said, "I'm no longer convinced that you can have the omni-inclusive church, you can have the one-size-fits-all church, or even the one-size-fits all denomination."[122] Hence, as the

---

[118] UUA Commission on Appraisal, *Engaging our Theological Diversity*, UUA, Boston, MA, May 2005, p. 1.
[119] Ibid.
[120] Ibid., p. 2.
[121] Ibid.
[122] Ibid., p. 2.

Commission's report concludes, "Despite consensus within the church that the liberal message of Unitarian Universalism is important in this troubled world, we find it difficult to articulate that message clearly."[123]

In his introduction to the 1999 Skinner House publication, *Redeeming Time: Endowing Your Church with the Power of Covenant*, editor Walter P. Herz says, "We too frequently behave as though Unitarian Universalism was born without historical or theological antecedents. We will continue to ignore our past only at the peril of losing our identity as a religious people."[124] Herz later adds that, "Theological diversity alone is an entirely inadequate basis for a strongly associated congregation of individuals, or for a truly functional association of congregations."[125]

Although this identity crisis has been made more apparent in recent years, especially in the 2005 Commission on Appraisal report, it was, to some extent, evident immediately following the merger. On its very eve in 1961, UUA leadership began an assessment of itself, the results of which were published just two years later in a report entitled, *The Free Church in a Changing World*. "What the report seemed to suggest," Robinson summarizes, "was a pattern of increasing religious pluralism, but a simultaneous need to discuss consensus, or identity, within that pluralism."[126] In the report's concluding remarks, Rev. Paul N. Barnes, who would later be elected President of the UUA, stated,

---

[123] Ibid., p. 3.
[124] Herz, Walter P., ed., *Redeeming Time: Endowing Your Church with the Power of Covenant*, Skinner House Press, Boston, MA, 1999, p. ix.
[125] Ibid, p. 117.
[126] Robinson, ibid., p. 175.

"religious liberalism has little to meet the challenge of today's need, or win our own personal need, if all it offers is a casual 'Join us and you can believe anything you want to'—as if religious convictions were to be left to such ephemeral judges as whim and wish!"[127]

This identity crisis is compounded by the difficulty many Unitarian Universalists have describing their religion to curious outsiders. "Is that the same thing as the Unity church?" They might ask. Or, "Isn't that the religion that believes everything?" This inability to understand who we are, largely because we don't recall who we were before the merger, perhaps in an attempt to avoid the historic, if not irreconcilable, conflicts between Unitarianism and Universalism, further explains our denomination's classification as a New Religious Movement.

NRM is the acronym used to describe our faith in the most recent American Religious Identification Survey (ARIS), conducted by Trinity College. The survey tracked "changes in the religious loyalties of the U.S. adult population within the 48 contiguous states from 1990 to 2008."[128] As an NRM, Unitarian Universalism is listed among Scientology, New Age, Eckankar, Spiritualist, Deist, Wiccan, Pagan, Druid, Indian Religion, Santeria, and Rastafarian, together representing only about 1.2 percent of the U.S. population. Of the 54,461 people surveyed in 2008, only 192 identified as UUs. It's difficult to know which is more troubling, that we are so numerically insignificant in America's religious landscape or that academia now

---

[127] Ibid.
[128] Barry A. Kosmin and Ariela Keysar, *American Religious Identification Survey (ARIS 2008)*, "Summary Report," March 2009.

considers Unitarian Universalism a new religion, severed from the ancient and rich history that once bound Unitarians and Universalists to their respective pasts.

4. An Association of Unitarians and Universalists

If the ultimate goal of the merger was to establish a universal religion of humanity beginning with the Unitarians and Universalists, as an exemplar to other liberal religions that might also wish to join forces with such a cooperative, the UUA could have remained an Association of both Unitarian and Universalist congregations, rather than morphing into a single religion that had never existed before and has remained ill-defined ever since. In his 2004 sermon, *Why Unitarian Universalism is Dying*, Rev. Davidson Loehr called "'Unitarian Universalism,' a religion that had never before existed anywhere, and to which no one of any note in history had ever belonged."[129]

The cumulative impacts of this identity crisis have resulted in the denomination's current identitarian paradigm, reinforced through its linguistically restrictive philosophies of safetyism and political correctness.[130] As a result, some may question my choice of the word "crisis" to describe the UUA's current milieu, given these suppressive social technologies have been largely successful in quieting dissenters, along with any other controversial voices. So, within its echo chamber of returning assent, all may seem calm in Boston. "The UUA advertises that it is a home of the

---

[129] http://austinuu.org/wp2011/why-unitarian-universalism-is-dying/
[130] For an in-depth discussion of these terms, see my previous essay, *The Coddling of the Unitarian Universalist Mind*, in this same volume.

free mind," complains Michael Werner, a former President of the UU Humanist Association, "but what is not said is that it is not home for free speech. Everyone knows the unspoken rule today is of going along to get along, so self-censorship is the real rule; think about it, just don't say it unless it is some nice comforting platitude."[131]

With this essay, however, it is my intention to burst this bubble in the hope of igniting genuine dialogue, encouraging others who share similar concerns to speak freely and openly and realize they are not alone, and to petition our UUA leadership to make better use of the sound reason, critical thinking, and introspection our faith, especially, is supposed to be committed to and capable of.

Yet I also wish to acknowledge, while it is often difficult to see the forest for the trees, our work is always deep down in the woods, amidst the countless trees where life occurs. Therein lies much uncertainty over which paths to take and which unknown territories to venture into, as well as many unforeseen obstructions and dangers. In the realm of living, confusion abounds. Nobody is to be blamed for getting lost from time to time during the journey.

Still, we are not without a guiding light. It is our faith that allows us to recall the larger vision of the forest, to see the bigger world through its lens, helping us through its dark nights as, with each step, we remember its grandeur and recall ourselves in the process. We remember who we are and what we're about. We remember our roots, those who have gone before us, where we come from, and the direction we now must take. Along the way an ancestor's voice

---

[131] Werner, Michael, *Regaining Balance: The Evolution of the UUA*, Religious Humanism Press, Hamden, CT, 2013, p. 56.

reminds us, "humanity lives both in and above history. We are fatefully caught in history, both as individuals and as members of a group, and we are also able to be creative in history."[132] It was this same forebear, the great Unitarian theologian James Luther Adams who also cautions that "only where there is the recovery of depth, breadth, and length, only there is the authentic spirit of religious liberalism to be found."[133]

With this in mind, the great difficulty for the new religious movement ours has become, this blended religion now called *Unitarian Universalism*, is that its merger has uprooted it from the unique and established histories of its namesakes. Nor, as an NRM, has it ever adequately dealt with the conflictive differences between them. The merger has not successfully reconciled their disparate theological traditions, nor has it ever even tried. Like most liberal organizations, it has also failed to address the larger and underlying issues of class that continue dividing our human family at large. Instead, it has now fallen under the spell of identity-based ethics, politics, and liberalism. By retreating into Identitarian Segregationism, which may be a more apt name for what it has become, Unitarian Universalism also severs itself from the one shared taproot that brought us together to begin with, the recognition that all people share a common humanity and we must, therefore, continue working together as one united family, no matter our differences.

---

[132] Adams, James Luther, *On Being Human Religiously*, Stackhouse, Max L. ed., Beacon Press, Boston, MA, 1976, p. 48.
[133] Ibid., p. 12.

So, without our ancient devotion to the shared calling that once bound these two traditions together, and with no other agreed upon or unifying purpose left between us, perhaps it's best to call it quits, while there's still a chance we can pick up the pieces of our individual lives as Unitarians and Universalists. Though, in honesty, I have little hope there is enough left of its former self for the latter to ever recover. For Universalism's original identity, in particular, has most easily been parasitized by today's identitarian wave. Its noble goal of uplifting the dignity of all human beings is easily confused with and, hence, co-opted by identity politics, or, as Francis Fukuyama prefers, "the politics of resentment."[134]

It also remains doubtful Universalism's pre-merger Judeo-Christian tradition, its faith in Jesus, or its belief in universal salvation will still resonate with more than a few remnants after a denominational split. On the other hand, Unitarianism's historic commitment to reason, freedom of conscience, and our common humanity are part of what draws and holds many individuals to Unitarian Universalism even now, though the UUA itself pays little homage to these cherished principles. Indeed, many are likely to become deeply troubled upon learning of the UUA's deviation from these core values and will seek an alternative, either by demanding institutional change, or deciding to abandon a faith that has abandoned them. For these, I hope a renewed commitment to Unitarianism alone will be a better alternative, along with the formation of a new association of Unitarians, including individuals and their communities, that

---

[134] Fukuyama, ibid., p. 7.

can finally move forward toward our common goals because we have reconnected with our historic past.

As in many a marriage, it is possible to initially be drawn together by a shared passion, to marry because of common interests, to share many years of happiness together, but to eventually grow apart, realize the relationship isn't working anymore, and to finally break up, hopefully departing as friends. I suggest that time has come for our denomination, and, with this essay, propose its members begin seriously discussing the dissolution of the UUA.

LET'S BE REASONABLE

A Rational Frame Regarding Charges of Racism and White Supremacy Within the Unitarian Universalist Association

1. Elementary

There is a major conflict within the Unitarian Universalist Association and its member congregations stemming from a March 2017 hiring decision. Some view the organization's decision to hire a white male candidate instead of a Latina candidate for one of its leadership positions a result of the liberal religion's culture of white supremacy. The other side, which has remained mostly muted, if not suppressed, wonders if the decision was based on the prospective employees' qualifications rather than her race, and if the unexpected appropriation of the term "white supremacy" to describe UUA culture isn't extreme. Evidence for the first argument boils down to (1) the rejected candidate's written recollection about comments made to her by UUA officials during her job interview, (2) her own assertion that she was qualified for the position, (3) as well as statistical data indicating the predominantly white staff already occupying leadership positions within the organization. There is no hard evidence for the dissenting argument since it would be unethical and sometimes unlawful for employers to publicly discuss or release private information about their employees, including prospective employees. This lack of evidence alone, however, is enough to lead some to conclude they must reserve judgment until more is known. For some, associating an organization like the UUA with white supremacy, furthermore, seems extreme enough to call the soundness of the entire position into question.

The matter could be resolved with the introduction of sound evidence proving the UUA excludes nonwhites due to institutional racism stemming from its culture of white supremacy. At this point, however, the one-sided evidence that's been presented remains inconclusive. The rejected applicant's account of statements made during a private job interview remains only a fraction of all that must have been said, is subjectively biased, and has not been, and is unlikely to be, confirmed or countered by her interviewers. The statistical data accompanied by her complaint, while concerning, to say the least, leads only to faulty reasoning if it remains unlinked to any specific systems that intentionally or unintentionally exclude qualified nonwhite employees.

It would, however, be faulty reasoning to suggest institutional racism rooted in the larger culture of 500-year-long white supremacy doesn't exist within the UUA, or doesn't influence its hiring practices, just because such direct evidence has not been presented. In logic, the suggestion something isn't true because it hasn't been proven, or, conversely, something is true because it hasn't been disproven, is a fallacy of Defective Induction called *ad ignorantiam* (argument from ignorance). Some might argue the numbers are proof enough, but, again, from a logical standpoint, numbers and statistics are consequents not causes. Using statistics alone to prove a point is to commit a *non-sequitur* known as, "affirming the consequent."

I'll show why this is fallacious momentarily, but, for now, I call upon us, as Unitarian Universalists, to be reasonable with each other. The Unitarian side of our religious tradition was founded upon freedom of conscience, human agency, and reason, which requires us to delve deeply into our own thinking to avoid the "idolatries of the mind and spirit." Reason requires us to be honest with each other, and to be honest with ourselves. It requires us to listen to each other, which means we must be allowed to share what we think without worrying that our language be perfectly acceptable before we speak.

Thus, while many consider logic to be cold and uninspiring, if not spiritually void, being reasonable is both compassionate and just. As retired professor of philosophy, Dr. Wallace Roark says in his book on logic, *Think Like an Octopus*, "The reason behind many bad things that happen in the lives of individuals and society can be expressed in the words of a blundering friend of mine, 'I just didn't think about *that*.' We have a moral and social, as well as prudential, obligation to think about *that*."[135] Or, as social psychologist Erich Fromm once wrote, "Thinking is a form

---

[135] Roark, Wallace, *Think Like an Octopus: The Key to Becoming a Good Thinker*, Wasteland Press, Shelbyville, KY, 2010, p. 21.

of productive love,"[136] and its function "is to know, to understand, to grasp, to relate oneself to things by comprehending them."[137] Being reasonable, in short, is a way for us to love one another.

2. Affirming the Consequent

Being reasonable gives us three choices when considering the value of an argument; (1) to determine it is valid and sound (if it's a deductive argument) or probable (if it's an inductive argument), (2) to determine it is invalid and unsound, or improbable, or, (3) to reserve judgment if there isn't enough evidence to make a reasonable determination. During its 2017 General Assembly in New Orleans, which occurred in the aftermath of the March 2017 decision, UUA delegates voted to perform an audit of its hiring practices to better determine the precise causes of the racial disparities among UUA employees, especially regarding those in leadership positions. (I will discuss some of its conclusions later.)

Rather than reserving judgement until more information was availed, a series of explicit and implicit false arguments rooted in the fallacy of *affirming the consequent* immediately transpired. Forgoing an unnecessary academic explanation of logical form, let's consider just one example that should make the problem with this fallacy obvious:

---

[136] Fromm, Erich, *Man for Himself: An Inquiry into the Psychology of Ethics*, Henry Holt & Company, New York, NY, 1947, p. 96.
[137] Ibid., p. 102.

> *If* it is a rainbow, *then* it has the color purple.
> The bouquet has the color purple.
> Therefore, the bouquet is a rainbow.

In this hypothetical argument, "has the color purple," is its consequent. Since the second line of the argument *affirms* the bouquet "has the color purple," it *affirms the consequent*. It's that simple. In such arguments the only valid way of dealing with the consequent is to deny it, as in the following example:

> *If* it is a rainbow, *then* it has the color purple.
> The silver disk in the sky *does not* have the color purple.
> Therefore, the silver disc in the sky is not a rainbow.

In this case, the second line *denies* the silver disc in the sky "has the color purple," proving, necessarily, it is not a rainbow. Now let's consider a couple more relevant examples:

> If one was a terrorist responsible for the attacks of 9/11, then one was a Muslim.
> Chris is a Muslim.
> Therefore, Chris is a terrorist responsible for the attacks of 9/11.

Since the second premise of this argument *affirms the consequent* by stating "Chris is a Muslim," it is invalid. If it were to deny the consequent by stating, "Chris is not a Muslim," we could rightly conclude this individual was not responsible for the attacks of 9/11, but nothing more about

Chris. Now let's consider an argument with the same form but with a different subject and predicate:

> If one is a White Nationalist, then one is white.
> Alex is white.
> Therefore, Alex is a White Nationalist.

By now the fault in this line of reasoning should be obvious. Yet this formal fallacy has been frequently committed during our current denominational crisis. The first such argument stems from a public statement issued on social media by the individual who was not hired for the UUA position, in which she asks, "…ultimately how do we hold the UUA accountable for racial discrimination and upholding white supremacy if no one stands up in the public square and says 'me, it was me, you did this to me and it is not ok, I demand you make this right!'"[138] In addition to committing a *fallacy of presumption* with a *complex* (alt. loaded) *question* (hiding a statement within a question), this statement *affirms the consequent* by insinuating that not getting the position is enough to prove her point.

As understandably painful and personal as the matter obviously is for this individual, being reasonable also requires us to consider the truth value of her statement, especially given its impact on our denomination. To allow ourselves to be solely convinced by our sympathies, however, is itself a kind of logical fallacy called *ad misericordiam* (appeal to pity). As philosopher, Jamie Whyte explains in his book, *Crimes Against Logic*, "Moral

---

[138]https://uuchristinarivera.wordpress.com/2017/03/27/on-being-a-good-fit-for-the-uua/

outrage at someone's mistreatment does not oblige you to agree with everything [one] says... this immunity from criticism cannot have the source many of its advocates allege it to: namely, that truth is culturally relative."[139] A compassionate response requires us to attend to the pain of others while remaining reasonable and reserving judgement until the necessary evidence is available to do more.

In this case, the statement made by the rejected job applicant suggests she wasn't hired because she is nonwhite, or, perhaps, that the UUA had a moral obligation to hire her because she is nonwhite,[140] and hiring a white person, especially a "white male" person, as she points out, is all the evidence necessary for us to conclude the organization "upholds white supremacy." Here's how the argument looks in logical form:

> If it upholds white supremacy, then it doesn't hire nonwhites for leadership positions.
> The UUA didn't hire a nonwhite for a leadership position.
> Therefore, the UUA upholds white supremacy.

As I've presented it, this argument is another example of the fallacy of *affirming the consequent*.

Around the world societies have developed different criteria for discriminating against others. For some it has been economic class, for some it has been caste, for some

---

[139] Whyte, Jamie, *Crimes Against Logic*, McGraw-Hill, Great Britain, 2005, p. 153f.

[140] I personally believe this is true, that we have a moral obligation to give special advantage to those who have historically been unjustly disadvantaged in our society. This, I believe, should be done with intention and transparency as a written policy of the UUA.

religion, and, here in the U.S., such discrimination has largely been based on [the fallacy of] race,[141] where it has been the privilege of whites to discriminate against nonwhites, leading to hundreds of years of genocide, slavery, inequality, segregation, poverty, police brutality, mass incarceration, and all the other horrors of injustice that go along with such cruelty and bias. Hence, it's understandable that many of us cannot help but associate such discrimination with "whiteness," including many whites troubled by their own feelings of shame and guilt. Nevertheless, it's about as reasonable to conclude being white automatically makes one a racist as it is to conclude being Muslim makes one a terrorist, or to conclude a mostly white organization is white supremacist as it is to conclude a Muslim organization must be a terrorist organization. Here's another contextual example of this fallacy:

> If it is a White Supremacist organization, then it is predominantly white.
> The UUA is predominantly white.
> Therefore, the UUA is a White Supremacist organization.

and another;

> If it is institutionally racist, then it will have a disproportionate number of white employees.

---

[141] I do not include gender in this list only because discrimination against women is so ubiquitous that it exists everywhere. According to the most recent United Nations data, which includes all 196 countries and territories in the world, though some are doing better than others, there is no place on Earth were women are treated equally to or are better off than men.

> The UUA has a disproportionate number of white employees.
> Therefore, the UUA is institutionally racist.

This is not to suggest some or all the propositional statements in these arguments aren't true, only that they are logically invalid because their conclusions do not follow from their premises. Here's an example of an invalid argument composed entirely of statements we can all agree are true:

> If it is a white supremacist organization, then it is predominantly white.
> The KKK is predominantly white.
> Therefore, the KKK is a white supremacist organization.

Although each of the three propositional statements comprising this argument can be considered true, the conclusion simply does not follow from its premises because, again, it commits the fallacy of *affirming the consequent*. In the case of the KKK, however, being predominantly white is the consequence of several causes that are easily explicated. Here's an example of a conditional argument that makes the point and is sound because, rather than making the mistake of affirming the consequent, it correctly *affirms the antecedent*:

> If an organization espouses a philosophy of white superiority and has a history of racist behavior against nonwhites, then it will be predominantly white.
> The KKK espouses a philosophy of white superiority and has a history of racist behavior against nonwhites.

Therefore, the KKK is predominantly white.

In the same way, to rightly conclude the UUA is institutionally racist, or upholds systems of white supremacy, we need to consider premises, if there are any, from which these conclusions logically follow. In short, we need to explicitly point out what those systems are. Determining these conclusions must be true based solely upon the "whiteness" of the organization's demographics is as faulty, and, I would argue, unjust, as determining all Muslims must be terrorists or that all mosques are terrorist organizations.

3. Affirming the Antecedent

In the kind of hypothetical (alt. *conditional*) arguments explored thus far, the term or phrase following the word, "if," is called the *antecedent*, and the term or phrase following the word, "then," is the *consequent*. For example, in the sentence, *If it is a dog, then it probably barks*, "it is a dog," is the antecedent and, "it probably barks," is the consequent (barking is a consequent of being a dog). In an argument using such a statement as its major premise, *affirming the consequent*, as we have seen, is always invalid. For example:

> If it is a dog, then it probably barks.
> The sealion barks.
> Therefore, the sealion is a dog.

An argument that *affirms the antecedent*, conversely, is always valid:

If it a dog, then it probably barks.
Daisy is a dog.
Therefore, Daisy probably barks.

In the same way, to correctly argue the UUA has racist hiring practices and upholds white supremacy, the antecedents (conditions) leading to these racist consequences must be affirmed. The systems that lead to such racial disparity, that is, ought to be made explicit so they can be reasonably considered. Here's an example:

If an organization has a policy against hiring nonwhites for top management positions, then it will not hire a candidate of Asian heritage as its next CEO.
Scourge Inc. has a policy against hiring nonwhites for top management positions.
Therefore, Scourge Inc. will not hire Sydney Jones, who is of Asian heritage, as its next CEO.

In this example, the antecedent, *an organization has a policy against hiring nonwhites for top management positions*, is the explicit cause of Sydney Jones being turned down for the job. These days, however, it is unlikely any organization would maintain explicit policies against hiring nonwhites for management or leadership positions. Since the Civil Rights Act was passed in 1964, racism in the U.S. has become, as sociologist Eduardo Bonilla-Silva says, largely "color blind," meaning it is no longer expressed in overtly racist terms. This makes it exceedingly difficult to prove whether such decisions are racially motivated or not. For, as Bonilla-Silva says, "in the postmodern world few claim to be 'racist' except for Nazis and Neonazis and members of white supremacist groups,"[142] resulting in what he terms a "new racism" through which white supremacy is "reproduced in a mostly institutional and apparently nonracial manner that relies on the *token inclusion*—rather than on the systematic exclusion—of racial minorities from certain jobs and places and does not depend on overt expressions of racial hostility."[143]

Hence, instead of Jim Crow laws, "whites only" signs, or using racist epithets outright, Bonilla-Silva's research identifies four dominant frames expressing racist attitudes through today's color-blind language. These include 1) *Abstract liberalism*, by which one claims to be against affirmative action, desegregation in education and housing, busing, interracial marriage, etc., etc., in an "abstract and decontextualized manner,"[144] such as, "I'm all for fairness and equality, which is why I don't think anyone should get special treatment;" 2) *Bioligization of culture*, by which nonwhites, especially blacks, are considered inferior because of some defect in "their" own culture, (i.e., because they are "lazy," "dependent," "criminal"); 3) *Naturalization of matters that reflect the impacts of white supremacy*, expressed, for example, by the opinion that neighborhood and social segregation is a choice made by nonwhites themselves because people prefer to be with "their own kind;" and, (4) *Minimalization of racism and discrimination* by claiming racism is on the decline, that few racist

---

[142] Bonillo-Silva, ibid., p. 140.
[143] Ibid., p. 67.
[144] Ibid.

structures still exist, and of reverse discrimination against whites.

Since neither the UUA, as an organization, or Unitarian Universalists, as individuals, generally speaking, use color blind racism to disguise racist sentiments, it is not reasonable to conclude it is a racist organization, at least according to Bonilla-Silva's four linguistic indicators. In other words, it is not possible to affirm that *Abstract Liberalism, Bioligization of Culture, Naturalization of matters that reflect the impacts of white supremacy,* or *Minimalization of racism and discrimination*, are promoted or expressed by the UUA or its members. Hence, if racism exists within the organization it is not the consequent of color-blind racism.

Nor are its employment statistics alone enough to reasonably conclude the UUA is systemically racist or white supremacist. Statistics are consequents of conditions that must be explicated. The question is not *what* are the statistics, by *why* are the statistics? An argument that claims they are the result of institutional racism rooted in a culture of white supremacy would be far stronger if those systems directly causing such disparity were affirmed. Having a largely white population doesn't necessarily make a group racist or white supremacist any more than being able to bark makes something a dog. Being a dog, on the other hand, enables most of them to bark, just as being a white supremacist group is the cause of such organizations having an exclusively white membership.

It takes more effort and time to draw logical links between such consequences and their potential causes—like race based gerrymandering, racist voter suppression laws, a racist criminal justice system, racially motivated disenfranchisement, racist lending practices, racist real estate practices, and racist social institutions that leave a disproportionate number of nonwhites in prison and poverty, and with poor access to quality jobs, housing, healthcare, and education—but, in the end, naming these causes, affirming these antecedents, is the only reasonable way to prove the conditions leading to undesirable consequences.

It should be noted, however, that denying the UUA is racist, systemically, or otherwise, because the conditions of such consequences are inconclusive would also be unreasonable. The point here is only that the conditions resulting in these disproportionate statistics must be made explicit (affirmed) before making logical inferences.

4. What Follows

Logic is sometimes referred to as "the study of what follows," meaning it's about drawing inferences from propositional statements (assertions of truth) serving as premises. If a conclusion logically "follows" from a premise, then the argument is sound. If it doesn't, whether the conclusion or its premises are true or not, the entire argument must be considered unsound.

In response to the conflict following the 2017 hiring decision, the UUA Board of Trustees created a Commission on Institutional Change:

> to work for a period of two years, in collaboration with a professional organization capable of conducting an external audit of white privilege and the structure of power within Unitarian Universalism, to analyze

structural racism and white supremacy within the UUA. The scope of the Commission shall be broad and far-reaching, with the goal of long-term cultural and institutional change that redeems the essential promise and ideals of Unitarian Universalism.

However one considers the immediate events leading up to the appointment of this Commission, it is reasonable to conclude the UUA, as part of a 500-year-old white supremacist culture in the U.S., no matter its internal values and intentions, remains influenced, to some extent, by racist systems and attitudes. As Bonilla-Silva says, "after a society becomes racialized, racialization develops a life of its own."[145] It is reasonable to expect any audits or reports the Commission produces should uncover some, hopefully many, even all, of the ways such racialization has developed a life of its own within the UUA. To be reasonable, its reports should identify "structural racism and white supremacy within the UUA," as reasons (premises) for concluding they result in racist consequences, including a disproportionate lack of nonwhites in leadership positions within the Association.

The six-person Commission appointed by the UUA Board of Trustees on June 21, 2017, issued a report on its "Findings Related to the Southern Regional Lead Hiring Decision, Spring 2017," in April of 2018. (It makes no mention of the "professional organization capable of conducting an external audit" it is supposed to have collaborated with.) One of its charges was to "Establish a 'truth and reconciliation' process to create a climate of

---

[145] Bonilla-Silva, ibid., p. 45.

honesty, accountability, and disclosure essential to our learning and multicultural growth as an institution." Instead, the report concludes that such a process is unlikely to work for the UUA because, "The time for 'reconciliation' may be passed." This is an alarming inference given that Truth and Reconciliation Commissions have been helpful in places like South Africa after decades of racist Apartheid, and in Rwanda after the Hutu majority brutally slaughtered up to a million people, and dismembered thousands more, during a hundred-day period of violence in 1994. What could the Commission on Institutional Change have uncovered within the UUA that is so much worse than these instances for it to conclude it's now too late for reconciliation to work for us?

The report acknowledges it is not "flawless," that "perfection" was not the Commission's intent, that it was completed within difficult time constraints, and that it was "conducted in good faith." Of course, the reason for its shortcomings are not pertinent to its value or its logic. If they are minor and clear enough, the report may nevertheless be, as the Commission hopes, "helpful." If they are severe enough, however, regardless of time constraints, good intentions, and hopes of the Commission, the report's usefulness becomes problematic. For it does not follow that a flawed report becomes valuable based upon difficulties and good intentions. These, rather, can only explain why it may be of little use, if any.

To complete the report, "The Commission on Institutional Change conducted 15 interviews and had a listening presence on a Board of Trustees conversation with former UUA President Peter Morales to grasp a range of perspectives related to the events around the Southern

Regional Lead Hiring decisions in the spring of 2017." Given that most interviewees were directly involved in or impacted by the "hiring decision" in question, the report explicates their sentiments about the matter but fails in its charge to uncover concrete "structures of racism and white supremacy within the UUA." Though it may represent only a step in this direction, as it stands, the report offers little more than information about the feelings and subjective experiences of those involved. The reader seems expected, that is, to draw objective conclusions about the UUA's "structures" based upon the largely emotional responses of those directly impacted by the situation in question. Relying on *ad populum* arguments (appeal to emotion) is a common informal fallacy. Objective conclusions do not follow from subjective premises.

Additionally, the report begins by stating its implicit bias regarding the issue it's supposed to be objectively exploring, reflecting the fallacy known as *begging the question*, in which the conclusion of an argument is already presented in its premises. As stated earlier, it remains unclear whether the hiring decision in question was the result of "structures of racism and white supremacy within the UUA," or due to legitimate issues with the applicant's credentials. The report, however, never considers the latter possibility. It states, rather;

> We begin with the premise in all our work that the values of Unitarian Universalism cannot be realized in a system which is centered around one cultural expression. In fact, the centering of white culture and values has stymied the development of a full range of

cultural expressions. In the Unitarian Universalist tradition, two "pillar" principles invite us to covenant to affirm and promote the inherent worth and dignity of all people and to acknowledge the interdependent web of existence of which we are all a part. Systems, policies, practices and expressions of Unitarian Universalism which bias one racial or cultural group above others make a mockery of these two core values and so we are called into efforts to name and change them as acts of witness to a fuller and more authentic expression of this faith.[146]

This bias, namely that the UUA is in violation of its own principles, as this hiring decision is presumed to prove, finds its confirmation throughout the report. On three occasions, for example, the report links the resignation of some UUA staff over the incident to the use of social media by others, as with the following example:

Resignations precluded the opportunity for further dialogue and full information disclosure. Instead the events were tried in the court of conjecture and social media.

Statements like this commit the fallacy known as *non causa pro causa* (no cause for cause), also known as *False Cause*. By linking two separate events together, this statement, particularly, implies they are causally related, that one logically follows from the other. Since it uses, "Instead," to bridge them together, it becomes a

---

[146] By already presuming the conclusion of its investigation, this statement is an example of the fallacy of *begging the question*, also known as circular reasoning.

disjunctive argument, meaning only one of two alternatives can be true; *Either* P *or* Q:

> *Either* there are no resignations and further dialogue, *or* events are communicated on social media.

By not explaining why turning to social media was the only alternative means of discussing the matter, the report may also present a *false dilemma,* meaning there may, indeed, have been other alternative means of communication available, or those who chose to use social media did so immediately and reactively without considering other options to begin with.

As stated, this disjunctive strongly favors those who "tried" the events "in the court of conjecture and social media," through the implication they were left with no other choice due to the actions of those whose, "Resignations compounded issues and did not allow an exploration through a more covenantal process as key actors were no longer available for dialogue." In short, statements like this blame the use of social media on those who resigned, though such a conclusion does not logically follow. This same bias is further expressed in statements like the following:

> Younger generations expect multicultural competency, are wary of institutions which lack authenticity with their values and expect more participatory models of shared leadership.

It would commit the fallacy of affirming the consequent to claim this statement alone suggests older generations of Unitarian Universalists don't share these same values. It may be true that younger generations have these values and expectations, that is, without mentioning the same is also true of existing older generations. In the context of the report, however, singling out younger generations implies they are different than older generations in these regards. Such ageism notwithstanding, many, if not most, Unitarian Universalists who have been around a while might argue against the implication they don't care about multiculturalism or shared leadership, two concerns that may well epitomize their values.

In addition to relying heavily upon sentiments and subjective accounts, the report is prone to criticizing the absence of systems, covenants, policies, procedures, and the like. Rather than uncovering and disclosing existing systems, that is, the report mostly criticizes the UUA for systems that don't exist. I will leave it to others to determine the value of such retrospective speculation. I will conclude this section, instead, by looking at the few existing structures it does explicate, (paraphrased and summarized by me) in the order in which they are presented in the report:

- There aren't enough people of color in positions of authority to influence the dominant culture of the UUA.
- Good governance practices were sometimes violated, and some rules were suspended by those in positions of power.

97

- The UUA allows the Board of Trustees and the President to take separate directions, making systemic changes difficult.
- Animosity between the Board of Trustees and the UUA President made cooperative efforts moving toward greater diversity nonexistent.
- The Board was not involved in or made aware of certain financial decisions.
- Hiring decisions are ultimately made by individuals not committees.
- Hiring decisions are inconsistent, undocumented, and informal.
- Legal concerns and lawsuits took precedence over the "covenantal values of our faith."
- There is a "lack of multicultural competency."

These nine statements, by my estimation, affirmatively explicate existing systems in the UUA, at least according to the report. Except for the first bulleted point, however, they are mostly unsubstantiated. The report states, "When the controversy began, of 56 people with supervisory responsibilities at the UUA, eight were people of color, or just over 14 percent…" According to the most recent Pew Research Center's *Religious Landscape Study* (2015) members among "Unitarians and other liberal faiths"[147] are 78 percent white, 9 percent Latino, 8 percent other or mixed, 5 percent black, and 1 percent Asian. These numbers are fairly consistent with the latest *American Religious Identification Study*, which further indicates the number of white members in the

---

[147] http://www.pewforum.org/religious-landscape-study/religious-family/unitarians-and-other-liberal-faiths-in-the-other-faiths-tradition/

UUA decreased from 90 percent to 75 percent between 1990 and 2008, as the number of nonwhite members has increased 11 to 25 percent, a 14 percent increase compared to an 11 percent increase during the same period in the U.S. population overall.[148]

If we are to determine employment parity within the UUA on basis of these statistics, the number of nonwhite employees with supervisory responsibilities must increase from 14 to 22 percent. By the same logic, 9 percent of these should be Latino, 8 percent other or mixed, 5 percent black, and 1 percent Asian. This kind of thinking also presumes white people are only willing to hire white people, and people of color are only willing to hire people of color, a conclusion that doesn't necessarily follow. It is also difficult to conclude an organization whose nonwhite membership and staff have both increased significantly in recent years upholds systems of white supremacy. Nor does any implication the UUA's racial demographics must correspond to those in the U.S. overall consider the cultural loyalties many nonwhites have toward other religions, (i.e., Catholicism, A.M.E., American Baptists, etc., etc.). In other words, UUA demographics may be the result of factors other than internal systems of racism and white supremacy.

Likewise, it does not follow that by suspending its own rules, or that a lack of transparency around some financial decisions, or that animus between its Board of Trustees and President, led to a racist hiring decision—dysfunctional a system as it might be. It should be noted, for example, were it not for the suspension of its rules, the

---

[148]https://commons.trincoll.edu/aris/files/2012/05/unitarians9008.pdf

rejected Latina candidate, who was a Board member herself at the time, would not have been able to apply for the position to begin with. Nor does it follow that such animus stifled racial progress within the UUA, as the report claims:

> This continued a pattern of animosity between the Administration and the Board which prevented a lack of clear vision on the steps needed for multicultural transformation…

This statement stands in contradiction to its additional claim that;

> The number of religious professionals of color has been growing, in part because of the support they get from UUA staff of color and because of the continued support for the annual gathering for religious professionals, "Finding Our Way Home" which was protected when other programs were cut by the administration of Rev. Peter Morales.

It does follow, however, that inconsistent, undocumented, and informal hiring decisions might lead to prejudicial treatment of some candidates, given there are no policies to help protect applicants from the potential biases of individuals making decisions entirely on their own. This seems to be a genuine issue that ought to be addressed. The complaint that hiring decisions are made by individuals, rather than by committees, on the other hand, seems a peculiar expectation. Although search committees are largely responsible for preselecting potential ministers in Unitarian Universalist congregations, it is not unusual for individuals to have the responsibility and authority to choose whom they determine to be the best candidate for a specific job. Hiring by committee is not a norm in the UUA. If it is to become so, a system will need to be put into place outlining how it is to work. Such a system, however, could cause new problems if those in supervisory positions don't have a strong voice in choosing the members of their staff.

As peculiar as this suggestion that hiring decisions should be made by committee comes across, it is far less so than the suggestion those with a fiduciary responsibility to the UUA should have ignored legal requirements and potential lawsuits in deference to the "covenantal values of our faith." This presents us with another false dilemma. For it is possible to be concerned about both, and, I would suggest, necessary. As a people of faith, Unitarian Universalists enjoy covenantal relationships among themselves and their ministers. But they must also involve themselves in contractual relationships, with outside organizations and paid staff, for instance. Perhaps, in this case, covenantal and contractual concerns came into conflict, but it does not follow that the only solution to this dilemma was taking the bull by the horns and breaking one of them off.

The final claim there is a lack of multicultural competency within the UUA goes unsubstantiated in the report, save for the anecdotal testimony from a few among the 15 people interviewed as the basis of its findings. There simply aren't enough facts to determine what level of such training or competency those involved in the 2017 hiring decision may or may not have had. Given the strong emphasis the UUA has placed on such training for many years, however, it is difficult to infer there wasn't at least some degree of multicultural awareness among those involved.

Unsubstantiated claims like this, which are supposed to serve as premises for its conclusions, are what makes the logic of this report difficult to follow and trust. We do not know the minds and hearts of those involved in the hiring decision. Nor have the, so called, "covenantal values" they were supposed to have upheld been spelled out for us. Was any such covenant even in place, and, if so, among whom? Unitarian Universalist congregations often have Covenants of Right Relations between their members, which usually include assumptions of best intentions and communicating directly with those with whom we may have conflict, at least to start with. Neither happened in this case. At one point the report itself violates these covenantal values by stating the 15 interviews it conducted revealed "the myriad ways that a system of sometimes unconscious (and sometimes conscious bias) white supremacy culture led to events which hurt many people, destabilized the workings and staffing at the UUA, and resulted in a less vital Unitarian Universalism."

In my analysis of the report, no such conclusion can logically be inferred. If this weren't problematic enough, its claim to know the "unconscious" bias of others, to read their minds, as it were, without substantiation for such an audacious statement, does not reflect the best of what

Unitarian Universalism is about and is disrespectful of those its authors presume to know better than they know themselves. Nor has the report logically confirmed its stated bias, that a "white supremacy culture led to events which hurt many people..." Its conclusion that things are so bad "the time for reconciliation may have passed" simply does not follow.

5. Definitions

It is also important to understand what we mean by the terms we use and how others take their meaning if we wish to be reasonable. Using terms in a way that is understood differently by others creates misunderstanding, which often leads to anger, disagreement, hurt, and separation. If the point is to be understood and to engage in productive dialogue, it is necessary to be clear about what we mean. Toward this end, it is beneficial to be familiar with the lexical definitions of the terms we use since these intentionally seek to avoid vagueness and outline the most commonly understood meanings of words.

Logic distinguishes between two kinds of definition, *intensional* (alt. connotative) and *extensional* (alt. denotative). *Intensional* definitions describe the attributes and characteristics shared by all objects, entities, or instances the general term being defined refers to. *Extensional* definitions attempt to get at the general meaning of a term by indicating specific examples of the objects, entities, or instances the term includes. Indicating groups like the Ku Klux Klan, Aryan Nations, Skinheads, White Nationalists, Neo Nazis, and the Alt-right to define *white supremacy* is

103

extensional. Defining it as, "The belief that white people are superior to those of all other races, especially the black race, and should therefore dominate society,"[149] as *Oxford Dictionary* does, is intensional. Understanding the intensional definition of a term allows us to determine its extension, but its extensional definition does not lead to its intension. If we attempt to determine the intention of *white supremacy* by looking only at the kind of groups previously mentioned, we might mistakenly infer it is only defined within a group context. Yet, as we have seen, the intensional definition just cited refers to it as a "belief" and doesn't reference groups at all.

Herein lies the first hurdle we must overcome before determining if it is reasonable to associate the UUA with white supremacy. Are we to take such an association to mean the UUA is to be grouped with the Ku Klux Klan, Aryan Nations, Skinheads, White Nationalists, Neo Nazis, and the Alt-right, as many would naturally presume? Or is the label meant to suggest the UUA holds the belief that *white people are superior to those of all other races, especially the black race, and should therefore dominate society*? Or is the assertion meant to imply both are true, that the UUA holds this belief and, thus, by extension, is a white supremacist group? It's often the case that intensional definitions are complimented with extensional examples, for the same

---

[149] Lexical definitions like this attempt to provide the most commonly understood meaning or meanings of a term, which is why its definition in the *Cambridge Dictionary* is similar; "The belief that people with pale skin are better than people with darker skin;" and why *Merriam-Webster* defines a *white supremacist* as, "a person who believes that the white race is inherently superior to other races and that white people should have control over people of other races."

reason a spelling bee contestant may ask for both a word's definition and its use in a sentence. Sociologist Nicki Lisa Cole illustrates this in her online article, *The History of White Supremacy: A Sociological Definition*:

> Historically, white supremacy has been understood as the belief that white people are superior to people of color. As such, white supremacy was the ideological driver of the European colonial projects and U.S. imperial projects: it was used to rationalize unjust rule of people and lands, theft of land and resources, enslavement, and genocide.[150]

Notice Cole's intensional definition is similar to the lexical definition cited earlier, though her extensional explanation points to examples of its social impact, not to specific groups that harbor the belief. If this is more akin to what those now associating the term with the UUA mean, then we must additionally ask if it is reasonable to associate the organization with unjust rule of people and lands, theft of land and resources, enslavement, and genocide?

Without taking time to go into detail about the UUA's history, values, and activism in the name of racial justice and equality, I will presume the reader knows enough about the organization to conclude none of these three meanings of white supremacy—(1) that it is a belief white people are superior to all others, (2) that it is a group like the KKK, Aryan Nations, Skinheads, White Nationalists, Neo Nazis, and the Alt-right, or (3) that it engages in the unjust rule over people and lands, steals land and resources, enslaves others, and commits genocide—apply to it.

---

[150] https://www.thoughtco.com/white-supremacy-definition-3026742

Concluding the UUA is associated with white supremacy does not logically follow from these definitions.

6. Disagreements

Logic also distinguishes between three kinds of disagreements, *obviously genuine*, *merely verbal*, and *apparently verbal but really genuine*. Disputants with an *obviously genuine* disagreement disagree even when they have the same understanding of the terms involved (i.e., one side believes in *Global Warming*, the other does not). Disputants with an *apparently verbal* disagreement aren't using the terms involved in the same way but would agree if they understood each other's meaning. Disputants with an *apparently verbal but really genuine* disagreement may think their misunderstanding will be resolved by clarifying their language but, upon doing so, discover their disagreement is about more than just wording.

If those involved in the disagreement over associating the UUA with white supremacy agree about this term's meaning, that it is a belief white people are and should be superior to all others, and/or is a group that practices this belief, and/or uses this belief to justify cruelties like inequality, slavery, and genocide, then the disagreement is *obviously genuine*. If the disagreement is *apparently verbal*, then there must be another definition of *white supremacy* we've not yet considered. If so, once considered, we will be in a good position to determine if the disagreement is, indeed, merely verbal, or if it is *apparently verbal but really genuine*.

In 2011, the *International Journal of Critical Pedagogy* published an article espousing multicultural educator Robin DiAngelo's theory of "White Fragility."[151] In 2017 the UUA invited DiAngelo to offer a workshop on the subject at its General Assembly, which included the following description in the GA program:

> White Fragility is a state in which even a minimum amount of racial stress becomes intolerable, triggering a range of defensive moves, including argumentation, invalidation, silence, withdrawal. This workshop will provide the perspectives and skills needed for white people to build their racial stamina and create more racially just practice.

Since then, The UUA's Beacon Press has published a bestselling book based upon DiAngelo's 2011 paper, successfully entrenching the meme of White Fragility into American nomenclature.

In a 2017 article on the subject, entitled, "No, I Won't Stop Saying, 'White Supremacy,'" DiAngelo suggests any disagreement over the term is merely verbal. "If it surprises and unsettles my audience that I use this term to refer to us and not them, [to "white progressives" and not "hate groups"] even after I have explained how I am using it, then they have not been listening."[152] This statement suggests the author's intention to clarify what she means by the term "white supremacy," and her conviction the dispute

---

[151] DiAngelo, Robin, "White Fragility," *International Journal of Critical Pedagogy*, Vol 3 (3) (2011) pp 54-70.
[152] "No, I Won't Stop Saying 'White Supremacy,'" by Robin DiAngelo — YES! Magazine, 7/19/2017

is merely verbal since she claims the only reason anyone might disagree with her is because they've not understood her definition of the term.

To substantiate her argument, she begins by tackling objections to the extensional definition of the term. "Many, especially older white people,[153] associate the term white supremacy with extreme and explicit hate groups. However, for sociologists, white supremacy is a highly descriptive term for the culture we live in; a culture which positions white people and all that is associated with them (whiteness) as ideal."[154] In this attempt to clarify her use of the term, DiAngelo demonstrates an informal fallacy known as *converse accident* (alt. *hasty generalization*). Simply put, this fallacy assumes what is true in a few instances is true in general. For, by speaking categorically of "sociologists," without specifying whether she means *some* or *all* of them, her reader is left to presume sociologists, in general, agree with her definition of white supremacy as a "highly descriptive term for the culture we live in; a culture which positions white people and all that is associated with them (whiteness) as ideal." If this is so, then sociologists, as a class, hold a definition that is different from the common understanding and use of the term as defined in most dictionaries. Yet, as we have already seen, at least one sociologist, Nicky Lisa Cole, uses the common lexical

---

[153] One's expertise in an area may often be enough to make a proposition more probable than not. Still, her claim this is true of, "Many, especially older white people," would be stronger if the reader could be sure it's based on statistical evidence and research, and isn't merely anecdotal on the part of the author.
[154] DiAngelo, ibid.

definition to define the term, not the definition DiAngelo argues belongs to sociologists in general.

Likewise, in his book on the subject, *White Supremacy & Racism in a Post-Civil Rights Era*, sociologist Eduardo Bonilla-Silva defines the term to mean, "racially based political regimes that emerged post-fifteenth century."[155] This definition could easily lead to Cole's examples of extension, though, like DiAngelo's, does not reflect the common lexical understanding, which may be why Bonilla-Silva admits he's, "fully cognizant it raises some questions."[156] He further argues the "institutionalist"[157] definition of white supremacy and racism, which argues, "racism is societal and implicates all white Americans,"[158] (akin to DiAngelo's definition) is flawed and inadequate. Firstly, it considers racism, in his words, "a mysterious almighty notion... 'a racist attitude' that 'permeates the society, on both the individual and institutional level."[159] Secondly, by considering race "the sole basis of social division... it is so inclusive it loses its theoretical usefulness."[160] Thirdly, its "black-white division" excludes "'white' groups (e.g., Irish and Jews) as plausible racial actors who have shared racialized experiences," and excludes other racial minority groups, "notably Native Americans, Puerto Ricans, and Chicanos."[161]

---

[155] Bonillo-Silva, ibid., p. 11.
[156] Ibid., p. 19.
[157] Ibid., p. 26.
[158] Ibid.
[159] Ibid., p. 27.
[160] Ibid.
[161] Ibid.

Thus far, Bonilla-Silva's arguments against using an institutionalist framework for defining white supremacy and racism are critical of its tendency to overgeneralize (to commit the fallacy of converse accident). His fourth argument against this framework, which he calls "circular," is something logic more often refers to as the fallacy of "Begging the Question," (*petitio principii*) because the conclusion is already presumed to be true in the argument's premises. For, "Racism," he continues, "which is or can be almost everything, is proven by anything done (or not done) by whites... any action done by whites is labeled as racist."[162] In addition to being fallacious, Bonilla-Silva considers this mindset counterproductive, "for institutionalists... all 'whites' are racist and thus there is little room for coalition-building with white progressives."[163]

Eduardo Bonilla-Silva and Nicki Lisa Cole are two sociologists who differ with the definition of white supremacy that Robin DiAngelo claims is the one sociologists use; indicating she may be overstating her case. Additionally, DiAngelo herself admits, "when race scholars use the term white supremacy, we do not use it the same way as mainstream culture does."[164] In addition to overgeneralizing again, by implying all or most race scholars are in agreement on this matter and use the term the same way she does, we must also ask if it is reasonable to expect most people should not be confused by her admittedly unconventional, non-lexical use of the term? As already

---

[162] Ibid., p. 27f.
[163] Ibid.
[164] DiAngelo, ibid.

mentioned, DiAngelo begins her article with a conditional proposition:

> If it surprises and unsettles my audience that I use this term to refer to us and not them, even after I have explained how I am using it, then they have not been listening.[165]

Although this statement isn't exactly a *petitio principii*, it does prompt us to ask if it is true that the only reason individuals might be surprised and unsettled by her argument, once explained, is because they haven't heard it? Is it possible there are other explanations for such disagreement? Is it possible to hear DiAngelo's explanation of the term and still disagree with her? Logic suggests when a disagreement continues after a clarification of terms has been made, it is *apparently verbal but really genuine.*

7. Fallacies of Accident & Composition

When using the quantifiers, *all, none, some,* or, *some are not,* we are speaking *categorically.* Speaking categorically allows us to denote whether we are speaking universally about a class[166] of objects designated by a term (*all* or *none*), or about particular instances of that class (*some* or *some are not*). Failing to indicate whether we're speaking universally or particularly can lead to confusion, misunderstanding, and faulty reasoning.

---

[165] Ibid.
[166] In logic the term "class" refers to all the objects that have some specified characteristic in common.

When, for example, as cited earlier, DiAngelo says, "I use this term ("white supremacy") to refer to us and not them," we cannot be sure if she means *all* of "us" and *none* of "them," or only *some* of "us" and *some* "of them" *are not*. When, without quantification, she makes statements like, "for sociologists, white supremacy is...," or, "when race scholars use the term...," it's easy to infer she is speaking in general about *all* (or most) sociologists and race scholars, not just a few.

When speaking categorically it's important to be clear about these distinctions if we especially wish to avoid four common fallacies; *accident, converse accident, composition*, and *division*. Fallacies of *accident* occur when we fail to take anomalies or exceptions to the rules into account—when, that is, we fail to consider special (accidental) circumstances and instances. Fallacies of *converse accident*, as already noted, occur when we make hasty generalizations based on only a few instances or anecdotal evidence. Fallacies of *composition* occur when we attribute qualities belonging to the individual members of a class to the class as a whole. Fallacies of *division* occur when we, conversely, attribute qualities belonging to a class as a whole to its individual members.

When, for example, Georgetown University law professor, Preston Mitchum asserted, "All white people are racist,"[167] he used a categorical statement that's *universal* in its quantity ("All"), and *affirmative* in its quality ("are"). The opposite of this statement, therefore, must be *particular* ("some") in its quantity, and *negative* in its quality ("are

---

[167] "Georgetown Law prof: 'All white people are racist. All men are sexist,'" *The Washington Times*, July 25, 2017, by Douglas Ernst.

not"); "Some white people are not racist." These two statements are considered *contradictories* because they cannot both be true or false. If one is true, the other must be false. Thus, if Mitchum's categorical assertion is true, each person considered part of the class, "white people," must be racist. Since he doesn't clarify what he means by "racist," it's reasonable to presume he accepts a common definition. If so, we must infer he means every white person, without exception, has a belief in white superiority, and/or supports discriminatory social systems, and/or is prejudiced against nonwhites.

Disproving this claim requires only one exception. That is, the existence of one person in the class of "white people" who does not believe in white superiority, doesn't support racist systems, and isn't prejudiced against nonwhites, makes this proposition false. This, then, would make its contradictory necessarily true, that *some white people are not racist*. Presuming there are many exceptions to Mitchum's rule, he seems to have committed the fallacy of *composition* by attributing what is true of some of its members to the entire class of "white people." This mistake is the same as asserting all felines are tigers because some felines are tigers, or that cars are made of rubber because they have rubber tires.

When, by contrast, DiAngelo says, "*Many* people, especially older white people, associate the term white supremacy with extreme and explicit hate groups,"[168] she implies only *some* people ("many" as they might be). Since this statement is *particular* in quantity and *positive* in quality, its opposite is the *universal negative* proposition

---

[168] DiAngelo, ibid.

that, *no people, especially older white people, associate the term white supremacy with extreme and explicit hate groups.* Since it's easy to prove that at least some people do define the term by its extension, and since these two statements are contradictories, meaning both cannot be false, we must conclude DiAngelo's assertion here is sound.

The problem, however, is that it's too broad and vague a statement to make any valid inferences from. Its import to any argument is meaningless. The term, "many," does imply "some," but could refer to a few anomalies, to a significant minority, to a small majority, or to most everyone in the class. By referring, further, to "Many people," we must infer she means many from the class of *all people*, including people of all races, although, given the context of her article, this remains unclear. When specifying, "older white people," as a subclass of "people," furthermore, DiAngelo provides no statistical evidence or research supporting the claim. Thus, in addition to being unable to determine if she's referring to only a minority or majority of older white people, or how many likely exceptions there are, we cannot know if the claim is based on her own anecdotal experience, or upon research based data, or how dramatically the subclass of "older white people" actually differs in this manner from the larger class of "people." If she is speaking anecdotally, she further commits the fallacy of *converse accident* by making a generalization about an entire class based upon insufficient evidence.

Later in her article, when DiAngelo refers to "white people as a group,"[169] it is clear she is speaking universally of "white people," but, only as a group, and not as

[169] Ibid.

individuals in that group. In other words, we must be cautious not to commit the fallacy of *division* by assuming what may be true of the group is true of each member in the group. This error may lie at the heart of the current UUA conflict, given that some members presume associating the denomination with white supremacy means they, as individuals, must also be white supremacists.

8. Categorically Speaking

When using categorical statements—statements quantified, implicitly or explicitly, by "all," "none," "some," and, "some are not"—we are engaging in categorical arguments. Like all arguments, categorical arguments are composed of propositional statements. A propositional statement asserts something is true. Not all propositional statements are part of a logical argument, but all logical arguments are composed of propositional statements. Some of these serve as premises (the reasons explaining *why* something is supposed to be true) and some as conclusions (asserting *what* should be considered true). For propositional statements to be part of an argument, they must have the proper form and share some terms in common so that its conclusion logically follows from its premises. A group of statements making similar or different assertions are not necessarily part of an argument. (This paragraph is a good example of using propositional assertions to explain their function in logic without being part of an argument, without some serving as premises and some as conclusions. I'm not explaining why these statements are true, that is, I'm only asserting that they are true.) To better grasp how propositions should work in a logical argument, let's compare Robin DiAngelo's argument claiming the existence of *White Fragility* with Eduardo Bonilla-Silva's argument claiming the existence of *Color-Blind Racism*.

Robin DiAngelo's White Fragility

In her original article, *White Fragility*, published by the International Journal of Critical Pedagogy in 2011, DiAngelo includes approximately 175 (compound) propositional statements asserting something is true.[170] These statements are included in 25 paragraphs, along with 10 bullet points listing what DiAngelo proposes are "triggers" and "varieties of racial stress,"[171] leading to what she has coined "White Fragility:"

> White Fragility is a state in which even a minimum amount of racial stress becomes intolerable, triggering a range of defensive moves. These moves include the outward display of emotions such as anger, fear, and guilt, and behaviors such as argumentation, silence, and leaving the stress-inducing situation.[172]

Within this framework, she uses "white people," "whites," and, "whiteness," in categorical terms 143 times. 131 of these are without quantification, leaving the reader to presume she must be referring to everyone or everything included in these categories. Of the 12 times she does imply

---

[170] Most of these are compound propositions, meaning, if they were broken down to simple propositions their number would easily double.
[171] DiAngelo, "White Fragility," ibid., p. 57.
[172] Ibid., p. 54.

some but not *all* "whites" or "white people," she quantifies them with terms like "most," "many," and, "generally." In none of these 143 instances does she offer any data or statistics as evidence for her calculations.

Nevertheless, her 14-page article gives the appearance of being well researched and supported by its inclusion of a nearly 3-page bibliography and 48 parenthetical reference points throughout its body. Upon review, however, most the references cited are meant only to support the truth of propositions she's asserted without explaining why they should be considered true, without providing, that is, the premises leading to these assertions to begin with. For example:

> Omi & Winant posit the U.S. racial order as an "unstable equilibrium," kept equilibrated by the State, but still unstable due to continual conflicts of interests and challenges to the racial order (pp. 78-9).[173]

Although it may be that Omi & Winant give good reasons for this conclusion in their original work, here it appears only as an unsubstantiated proposition. DiAngelo's argument would be stronger if the reasons for this assertion were provided. She then uses this weakly substantiated concept to infer the following:

> When any of the above triggers (challenges in the habitus[174]) occur, the resulting disequilibrium becomes

---

[173] Ibid., p. 58.
[174] DiAngelo explains, "Bourdieu's concept of habitus (1993) may be useful here. According to Bourdieu, habitus is a socialized subjectivity;

intolerable. Because White Fragility finds its support in and is a function of white privilege, fragility and privilege result in responses that function to restore equilibrium and return the resources "lost" via the challenge—resistance towards the trigger, shutting down and/or tuning out, indulgence in emotional incapacitation such as guilt or "hurt feelings", exiting, or a combination of these responses.[175]

The "triggers" to which DiAngelo refers are a list of 10 bulleted assertions with no references or other evidence explaining why they should be considered true. Rather, her stated proofs for "this lack of racial stamina," which she's named, "White Fragility,"[176] may rely almost entirely upon her own anecdotal experiences—subjective experiences, that is, which she translates into objective conclusions about "whites," "white people," and, "whiteness," in general. Consider the following statements:

> ...whites are usually more receptive to validating white racism if that racism is constructed as residing in individual white people other than themselves.[177]

> Whites often confuse comfort with safety and state that we don't feel safe when what we really mean is that we don't feel comfortable.[178]

---

a set of dispositions which generate practices and perceptions." (Ibid., p. 58)

[175] DiAngelo, ibid.

[176] Ibid., p. 56.

[177] Ibid., p. 61.

[178] Ibid.

...it is rare for most whites to experience a sense of not belonging.[179]

In these examples, we don't know if DiAngelo's vague quantifications, "rare," "most," "usually," and "often," are substantiated by any statistical data beyond her own experiences and interpretation of the unconscious meaning of what others say. This is not to say such data doesn't exist, only that it has not been presented by her in this paper if it does.

As it stands, her article is comprised mostly of propositional declarations of truth the reader must accept based solely upon her expertise and the expertise of those she cites. While expertise can be a sound reason in favor of an argument, experts can be mistaken, often disagree with one another, and make only their best educated guesses. Thus, it is more reasonable to accept an expert opinion when it is supported with empirical proof, something lacking in DiAngelo's paper.

Even if her theory were correct, however, her use of it commits the fallacy of *affirming the consequent*. Even if "White Fragility" exists and results in anger, argumentation, shame, silence, and withdrawal, it does not mean a person who expresses any of these responses must have "White Fragility." There may be other reasons for having these kinds of emotional responses to such an accusation, which, after all, are the usual human responses to being insulted or offended.

With such little evidence for her theory, we are left with no sound reason to accept the existence of "White

---

[179] Ibid., p. 62.

Fragility." It may even seem dubious coming from one who has published a magazine article forthrightly refusing to stop using the term "white supremacy" to refer, implicitly, to *all* whites and *all* white people, including "older white people," [180] "those whites who marched in the 1960s Civil Rights movement,"[181] "many white liberals,"[182] and, "so-called progressive whites,"[183] whom she suggests can only disagree with her if "they haven't been listening." To further suggest those who do disagree must be suffering from a condition she herself has conceived, the symptoms of which are anger, argumentation, shame, silence, and withdrawal, leaves them with no option but to utterly agree with her, by which I mean, to vocally *utter* agreement or else be diagnosed with the condition. By merely pointing out the potential faults in such thinking, my criticism may itself be conveniently dismissed as symptomatic.

Eduardo Bonilla-Silva's Color-Blind Racism

In his well substantiated and well-argued book, *White Supremacy & Racism in the Post-Civil Rights Era*, socialist Eduardo Bonilla-Silva coins the term, "color-blind racism,"[184] by which he means racism that no longer depends "on overt expressions of racial hostility."[185] This new kind of racism, rather, "is anchored in the abstract extension of

---

[180] DiAngelo, "No, I Won't Stop Saying, 'White Supremacy,'" ibid.
[181] Ibid.
[182] DiAngelo, *White Fragility*, ibid, p. 54.
[183] Ibid., p. 55.
[184] Bonilla-Silva, ibid., p. 67.
[185] Ibid.

egalitarian values to racial minorities and on the notion that racial minorities are culturally deficient."[186] Hence, instead of posting "whites only" signs on public restrooms and pools, or enacting laws preventing nonwhites access to certain schools, neighborhoods, businesses, or occupations, today white supremacy is guised in language that sounds "reasonable" and "pragmatic."[187]

As an example of this, Bonilla-Silva provides a statement made by a human resource manager about school integration in U.S. schools. The individual, in her early fifties at the time, seems strained to articulate a sound reason for her expressed opposition to busing that doesn't sound overtly racist. Instead she speaks of the importance of "developing a sense of community," of just not wanting her children to be bused, the importance of kids learning to "make a life for themselves," and of "interaction between races," only to conclude her "abstract liberalism," as Bonilla-Silva calls it, with, "I'm just not a busing person."[188]

In this example, the individual doesn't use racist epithets or disparaging remarks against nonwhites, or say she is against "race-mixing," or for, "equal but separate." Instead she struggles to sound open and inclusive, as has become socially appropriate, while validating a system of segregation in schools without directly saying so. When it comes to integrated neighborhoods, this same individual says, "I don't have a problem with all white and all black

---

[186] Ibid.
[187] Ibid.
[188] Ibid. p. 67f.

neighborhoods... if that's the choice of the people, the individuals."[189] Here, again, rather than expressing the traditional racist ideology of segregation, or addressing the systems that still prevent many nonwhites from having access to affluent neighborhoods, the individual sounds as if she is upholding freedom and democracy, the right of people to live where they choose, because, as some would say, "people prefer to live with their own kind."

Pertinent to this work, these examples show how Bonilla-Silva offers examples serving as premises for his claim that racism has become color-blind. Indeed, he offers numerous similar examples throughout his book so that his readers are exposed to much evidence proving his points. His evidence is so plentiful he's able to narrow these collected sources down to what he calls, "four primary storylines," told by (some) whites;

1. "The past is the past." (alt. "Present generations are not responsible for the mistakes of the past.")
2. "I didn't own slaves."
3. "My [friend or relative] didn't get a [job or promotion] because a black [usually 'man'] got it."
4. If [Jews, Irish, Asians] have made it, how come blacks have not?"[190]

In addition to the prevalence of documented, though anecdotal, examples obtained from numerous interviews helping to support his points, Bonilla-Silva offers convincing statistical data that even more soundly makes his case. In 1998, for example, he was the principle investigator

---

[189] Ibid., p. 68.
[190] Ibid., p. 70.

on the Detroit Area Study on White Racial Ideology. The DAS survey included 400 Detroit metro-area residents (67 blacks and 323 whites). "The response rate was an acceptable 67.5 percent. As part of this study, 84 respondents (a 21 percent subsample) were randomly selected for in-depth interviews (67 whites and 17 blacks)."[191] The interviews were conducted for about an hour under specific protocols, and the responses were reported verbatim, including "nonlexicals, pauses, and meaningful changes in intonation."[192] Afterward, Bonilla-Silva says, "I read all the interviews to extract common themes and patterns."[193] These common themes are those mentioned in Section 3 of this article; *Abstract Liberalism, Bioligization of Culture, Naturalization on racial matters,* and *Minimalization of racism.*

The DAS research allowed Bonilla-Silva to calculate statistical data indicating the percentage of times these color-blind frames were used by his subjects. *Abstract Liberalism* was deployed most often by 35 percent of black interviewees compared to 96 percent of white interviewees; *Bioligization of Culture* was deployed by 24 percent of black interviewees compared to 88 percent of white interviewees. *Naturalization on racial matters* was also deployed by 24 percent of black interviewees compared to 43 percent of white interviewees, and *Minimization of racism* by only 6 percent of black interviewees compared to 84 percent of white interviewees.[194] Bonilla-Silva then goes into detailed

---

[191] Ibid., p. 140.
[192] Ibid.
[193] Ibid.
[194] Ibid., p. 142.

discussion of some of the responses leading to these statistics.

His work on the extremely important matter of racism and white supremacy in the U.S., which continues to detrimentally impact the lives of millions, is both theoretical and analytical, meaning he not only asserts what he believes to be true, he also includes convincing objective research and data as reasons backing his arguments. Even when suggesting something is true of *most* whites, he does so by providing statistical evidence to prove it.

To be reasonable, it is necessary to accept arguments that are well substantiated with sound research and evidence. Logic does not allow us to be persuaded by propositional assertions of truth without sound reasons for accepting them. Reason requires us to consider the margin of error in the thinking of others, as well as in our own, and to remember there are few, if any, absolutes in the world, and, thus, few reasons for certainty.

9. Conclusions

To be reasonable, the inferences and conclusions we hold must logically follow from our premises. They are not logical just because we want them to be, or because they come from people who have suffered, or because the person saying them holds the megaphone. Nor are those made by dissenting voices necessarily wrong because of their arbitrary genetic qualities, nor because we claim to know their hidden motivations, nor because they are inconvenient to our own narrative. Logic helps us see if the conclusions we draw are derived at objectively, according to proper form. It helps us see the error in our thinking, but, alas, cannot help us know if our conclusions are true. Truth is a perennial problem none of us has the right to claim, no matter how certain we feel; and certainty is never an excuse to silence others or stifle genuine dialogue.

Throughout human history the expression of displeasing ideas has been stifled, sometimes forcefully and violently, sometimes through fear and intimidation, and sometimes by taking advantage of the fundamental human need to belong and remain included in the good graces and company of others. Some have been forcefully silenced, while others have censored themselves to remain safe and in good standing. Whatever the reasons, it often seems better and easier to simply go along with the crowd than against it. Now cannot be such a time in the UUA.

I have little doubt the reasoning presented in this article will rub many among us the wrong way, some of whom may lash out against it, against me. This is so because we live in a culture these days in which many presume they have a right *not* to hear things they find disagreeable, that ideas and words are violent, and that it's okay to defend themselves and others against dangerous thoughts and beliefs by demonizing, calling out, shouting down, shaming, silencing, banishing, and sometimes physically assaulting those with whom they disagree. Such behavior has not, historically, been the way of Unitarians and Universalists. Nor has using social pressure and political maneuvering to suppress dissenting voices. Nor has it been our way to assume the worst intentions in others, nor to presume we have the magical power to read their minds. Nor have we ascribed to the Doctrine of Original Sin, the belief some people are born innately flawed, making it possible to categorically judge their hearts based upon their color, their gender, their sexuality, their generation. Nor has it been our way to be thoughtless by treating each other unreasonably.

Yet an honest discussion about what happened regarding the 2017 hiring decision and what it may imply about our religion has not occurred, it has been stifled. It is my hope, by stating what many may think but have been afraid to say, or have had no space to say, that others will be emboldened to speak their minds in good faith, and that those who have refused such dissent will open their hearts and minds to a conversation that still needs to occur if our denomination wishes to remain healthy and whole.

Admittedly, the logic I've expressed in this article may not be without error, and likely is not. I too am blinded by my emotions—the sadness, fear, and anger I sometimes feel about what's going on in my religion—no matter how much I've tried to remain objective by examining the logical form of the various arguments explored in this article. I too, no doubt, succumb to confirmation bias, leading me to address the flaws in the thinking I disagree with, while being unable to entertain its accuracies. But being wrong doesn't make one fundamentally flawed as a person, no more than being right makes one righteous. It's okay to express ideas that are wrong, just as it's okay to hear them. This, at least, has been the way of Unitarian Universalism in the past. I hope it has not become a part of our past. I hope we can still be reasonable.

AFTERWARD

It may be true that you can't legislate integration, but you can legislate desegregation. It may be true that morality cannot be legislated, but behavior can be regulated. It may be true that the law cannot change the heart, but it can restrain the heartless. It may be true that the law can't make a man love me, but it can restrain him from lynching me, and I think that's pretty important also.

Dr. Martin Luther King Jr. spoke these words during an April 5, 1965 speech at UCLA while calling for the passage of a voting rights act. King believed the problem of racial injustice in the United States requires legal solutions. This doesn't mean he didn't also grasp the moral and psychological roots of this struggle, only that he didn't confront the problem by pointlessly attempting to change or control the hearts and minds of millions of other people. He chose, rather, to impact large swaths of society by changing its rules, by working to level the playing field, by requiring people to treat one another with respect even if their inner selves have no such respect.

Today, however, too many of us, especially liberals, continue to consider racism a heart problem requiring a psychological solution; rather than establishing meaningful laws, policies, institutions, and systems that prohibit racist behaviors and systemic racism regardless of personal attitudes. As Bonilla-Silva complains, "Most analysts regard racism as a matter of individuals subscribing to an irrational view, thus the cure is educating them to realize that racism is wrong."[195]

Toward this end, identitarianism and its mounting list of technologies—political correctness, safetyism, microaggressions, misappropriation, concept creep, safe spaces, trigger warnings, virtue signaling, and, most recently, white fragility—enable novices to falsely believe they have the tools necessary for reading the minds of others and diagnosing the unconscious motivations of their hearts. Their haphazard insights, however, only perpetuate the very prejudices they seek to overcome.

If they should succeed in this, we are likely to end up with a society of people who don't make racist comments, not even color-blind comments, and has removed all its racist symbols and monuments, but, for all practical purposes, remains racist. According to the United Nations' list of social indicators, for example, nonwhites, especially African Americans and Latinos, are no better off in the U.S.

---

[195] Bonilla-Silva, Eduardo, ibid., p. 46.

today, in the areas of housing, education, health, and employment, as examples, than before the Civil Rights and Voting Rights acts were passed in the 1960s. This is so because the U.S., including the U.S. Supreme Court, continues conflating being racist with racism, heart with habit.

Today, there are many racists in the U.S. who have no power to engage in racism because they are powerless to establish racist systems. At the same time, there are many goodhearted individuals who are not racists, yet engage in racism daily because they are ensnared in age old systems of white supremacy. In both cases, attempting to solve the problem by changing individual hearts is largely futile. If we are ever going to finally end racism and white supremacy in the United States, we must address racism not merely racists. *We*, by whom I mean all of us who care, regardless of our individual identities, must do far more than signal our own virtues by publicly diagnosing others as fragile, pointing out their privilege, or magically, sloppily, and unethically mindreading their unconscious motivations. We must, instead, change the rules.

Again, as Bonilla-Silva points out, "blacks and most racial minorities lag behind whites in terms of income, wealth, occupational and health status, educational attainment, and other relevant social indicators."[196] He also says, "after a society becomes racialized, racialization develops a life of its own."[197] Hence, attempting to interpret and change individual hearts is pointless when systemic

---

[196] Ibid., p. 1.
[197] Ibid., p. 45.

racism continues ruining the lives of millions of nonwhites who deserve much better.

This is why, throughout my two decades of UU ministry, I have called for an end to the racially motivated drug war, for the establishment of a prison quota system that prohibits the disproportionate confinement of nonwhites, for an end to the punitive criminal justice system altogether, and for expunging the records of and making financial reparations to those unfortunate men and women swept up in, as Michelle Alexander so aptly names it, *The New Jim Crow*.

More than merely pounding the pulpit, however, I have also worked integrally with others to make these things happen. In 2008, for example, I was asked to chair a Restorative Justice committee on behalf of the Louisville Bar Association. Shortly thereafter, the Jefferson County Disproportionate Minority Confinement Advisory Board asked our diverse committee to create a pilot program for underaged offenders. We did, and today, without ever calling anyone out, or working to change a single heart, Louisville, Kentucky has a Restorative Justice program that successfully prevents young people from ever entering the school-to-prison pipeline.

Shortly after my move to Spokane in 2011 the opportunity arose to help promote the passage of a bill decriminalizing marijuana in Washington. Since Spokane County tends to vote more conservatively than most the State, it was necessary to provide educational opportunities about the initiative in our area if it was going to gain enough support to pass statewide. Some of the important work the Unitarian Universalist Church of Spokane engaged in to make this happen is presented in the documentary film, *Evergreen: The Road to Legalization*. Here I will point out that only six months after Initiative 502 was successfully passed the number of police stop-and-searches in Washington was cut in half, dramatically reducing the number of potentially dangerous encounters between law enforcement and some of its nonwhite citizens.

These are examples of what a few people from diverse backgrounds are able to accomplish together through issue-based activism rather than divisive identity politics. That the latter, by contrast, prefers a psychological solution to social problems, futilely attempting to force a change of heart by suppressing speech and controlling the larger mindset, is predictable. For prioritizing the dignity of individual feelings and one's lived experience, as Francis Fukuyama says, "turns the private quest for self into a political project..."[198] leaving little room for "perspectives and feelings that can be shared across group boundaries."[199]

Nor, in retrospect, should it be surprising Unitarian Universalists have fallen into the same trap other liberals have since losing political power and retreating into their own institutional lives in the 1980s and 90s. "The diminished ambitions for large-scale socioeconomic reform converged with the left's embrace of identity politics and multiculturalism in the final decades of the twentieth century," Fukuyama explains. "The left continued to be defined by its passion for equality, but that agenda shifted from its earlier emphasis on the conditions of the working

---

[198] Fukuyama, ibid., p. 37.
[199] Ibid., p. 111.

class to the often psychological demands of an ever-widening circle of marginalized groups."[200]

I do not believe relating to each other this way is tenable or sustainable for Unitarian Universalism. Either we reconnect with our historic roots, dealing, at last, with our theological and class conflicts, so we can return to and fulfill our promise of establishing a universal nonsectarian religion of humanity, or we allow our a misguided identitarian philosophy to continue segregating us from each other until all that remains necessary for the dissolution of our denomination is mere formality. I hope it doesn't come to this, but if it's the only way to remember and recommit to our once cherished principles of reason, freedom of conscience, and common humanity, we may have no other choice. If, however, there remains another choice, perhaps it is best expressed in the words of Dr. King: "A social movement that only moves people is merely a revolt. A movement that changes both people and institutions is a revolution."[201]

---

[200] Ibid., p. 113.
[201] King, Martin Luther, *Why We Can't Wait*, Signet Classic, New York, NY, 1964, p. 107.

SOURCES CITED

Adams, James Luther, *On Being Human Religiously*, 2nd edition, Stackhouse, Max L. ed., Beacon Press, Boston, MA, 1976

Appiah, Kwame Anthony, *The Lies that Bind*, Liveright Publishing Corporation, New York, NY, 2018

Barry A. Kosmin and Ariela Keysar, *American Religious Identification Survey (ARIS 2008)*, "Summary Report," March 2009

Berry, Wendell, *Sex, Economy, Freedom, and Community*, Pantheon, New York, NY, 1993

Bonilla-Silva, Eduardo, *White Supremacy & Racism in the Post-Civil Rights Era*, Lynne Rienner Publishers, Boulder, CO, 2001

Crowley, Tony, "Colonialism and Language," The
        Cambridge Encyclopedia of the Language Sciences,
        ed. P. Hogan, Cambridge, 2008

Devine, Philip E., *Human Diversity and the Culture Wars*,
        Praeger Publishers, Westport, CT, 1996

DiAngelo, Robin, "No, I Won't Stop Saying "White
        Supremacy," *YES! Magazine*, 7/19/2017

DiAngelo, Robin, "White Fragility," *International Journal
        of Critical Pedagogy*, Vol 3 (3) (2011)

Dietrich, John H., *What if the World Went Humanist? Ten
        Pulpit Addresses by John H. Dietrich*, The
        HUUmanists Association, Hamden, CT., 2010

Elshtain, Jean Bethke, *Democracy on Trial*, Basic Books,
New York, NY, 1995

Ernst, Douglas, "Georgetown Law prof: 'All white people
        are racist. All men are sexist,'" *The Washington
        Times*, July 25, 2017

Fox, Matthew, *One River, Many Wells*, Jeremy P.
        Tarcher/Putnam, New York, NY, 2000

Freedman, Russell, *Indian Chiefs*, Scholastic Inc., New
York, NY, 1987

Fromm, Erich, *Escape from Freedom*, Avon Books, The
        Heart Corporation, New York, NY, 1941, 1966

Fromm, Erich, *The Art of Loving*, (Harper & Row, New
York, NY, 1956

Fromm, Erich, *Man for Himself: An Inquiry into the Psychology of Ethics*, Henry Holt & Company, New York, NY, 1947

Frothingham, Richard, *A Tribute to Starr King*, Ticknor and Fields, Boston, MA, 1865

Fukuyama, Francis, *Identity: The Demand for Dignity and the Politics of Resentment*, Farrar, Straus and Giroux, New York, NY, 2018

Herz, Walter P., ed., *Redeeming Time: Endowing Your Church with the Power of Covenant*, Skinner House Press, Boston, MA, 1999

Holmes, John Haynes, *The Revolutionary Function of the Modern Church*, G.P. Putnam's Sons, New York, NY, 1912

Howe, Charles A., *For Faith and Freedom*, Skinner House Press, Boston, MA, 1997

http://austinuu.org/wp2011/why-unitarian-universalism-is-dying/

https://commons.trincoll.edu/aris/files/2012/05/unitarians9008.pdf

http://www.merriam-webster.com/dictionary/identity%20crisis

http://www.pewforum.org/religious-landscape-study/religious-family/unitarians-and-other-liberal-faiths-in-the-other-faiths-tradition/

http://www.thefreedictionary.com/identity+crisis

https://www.thoughtco.com/white-supremacy-definition-3026742

https://uuchristinarivera.wordpress.com/2017/03/27/on-being-a-good-fit-for-the-uua/

Irvine, William B., *A Guide to the Good Life*, Oxford University Press, New York, NY, 2009

Isabelle L'eglise, Bettina Migge, "Language and colonialism. Applied linguistics in the context of creole communities," Marlis Hellinger & Anne Pauwels. Language and Communication: Diversity and Change. Handbook of Applied Linguistics, Mouton de Gruyter, pp. 297-338, 2007

Kennan, George F., *Around the Cragged Hill*, W.W. Norton & Company, New York, NY, 1993

Lilla, Mark, *The Once and Future Liberal*, HarperCollins Publishers, New York, NY, 2017

Lukianoff, Greg and Haidt, Jonathan, *The Coddling of the American Mind,* Penguin Press, New York, NY, 2018

McDowell, Esther, *Unitarians in the State of Washington*, Frank McCaffrey Publishers, 1966

Miller, Russell E., *The Larger Hope: The First Century of the Universalist Church in America 1770-1870*, Unitarian Universalist Association, Boston, MA, 1979

Murray, John, *Record of the Life of Rev. John Murray, Monroe and Francis, Boston, MA*, 1816

Newman, Michael, *Socialism: A Very Short Introduction,* Oxford University Press, 2005

Pierce, Chester M., "Psychiatric Problems of the Black Minority," from *American Handbook of Psychiatry: Volume 2*, edited by Silvano Arieti, Basic Books, New York, NY, 1974

Roark, Wallace, *Think Like an Octopus: The Key to Becoming a Good Thinker*, Wasteland Press, Shelbyville, KY, 2010

Robinson, David, *The Unitarians and the Universalists*, Greenwood Press, Westport, CT, 1985

Rosenblatt, Helena, *The Lost History of Liberalism*, Princeton University Press, Princeton, NJ, 2018

Scott, Annie, "Post Fall Conference Message form the Board," Issued to the LREDA Membership, November 8th, 2017

Shook, John R., *The Dictionary of Modern American Philosophers*, Thoemmes Continuum, Great Britain, 2005

The Report of the Commission on Appraisal for the American Unitarian Association, "Unitarians Face a New Age," 25 Beacon Street, Boston, MA, 1936

UUA Commission on Appraisal, *Engaging our Theological Diversity*, UUA, Boston, MA, May 2005

Werner, Michael, *Regaining Balance: The Evolution of the UUA*, Religious Humanism Press, Hamden, CT, 2013

Whyte, Jamie, *Crimes Against Logic*, McGraw-Hill, Great Britain, 2005

Williams, George H., "American Universalism: A Bicentennial Historical Essay," The Universalist Historical Society, Raleigh, North Carolina, 1971

Winston, Carleton, *The Circle of Earth: The Story of John H. Dietrich*, G.P. Putnam's Sons, New York, NY, 1942

ABOUT THE AUTHOR

Rev. Dr. Todd F. Eklof is a former Southern Baptist minister who converted to Unitarian Universalism in 1988 and reentered the ministry as a Unitarian Universalist in 1999. In addition to serving as minister of Clifton Unitarian Church in Louisville, KY from 1999 to 2011, and minister of the Unitarian Universalist Church of Spokane since 2011, he had a sixteen-year career in television news and corporate video production. Rev. Eklof holds undergraduate degrees in Philosophy and Communications, a Master of Arts in Religions Studies, a Doctor of Ministry from Meadville Lombard Theological School, and is a certified member of the American Philosophical Practitioners Association (APPA). He is widely appreciated for his advocacy and activism in the areas of criminal justice reform, restorative justice, marriage equality, and environmental issues, and is founder of the Kerdcera Dojo, devoted to the practice of reason and emotional intelligence.